11.03 77 11/02

THE OUIJA® BOOK

Gina Covina

Simon and Schuster
New York

OUIJA and MYSTIFYING ORACLE
are the registered trademarks of Parker Brothers,
Beverly, Ma., for its talking board game equipment
and are used with permission but without
sponsorship or endorsement of this book.
Designed by Dianne Pinkowitz
Manufactured in the United States of America
Printed and bound by Fairfield Graphics, Inc.
1 2 3 4 5 6 7 8 9 10

Library of Congress Cataloging in Publication Data

Covina, Gina.
    The Ouija book.

    1. Ouija board.   I.   Title.
BF1343.C68   133.9'3   78–24571

ISBN   0–671–22840–4

ACKNOWLEDGMENT

THANK YOU

to the friends who sat at the OUIJA board with me and provided the practical experience upon which this book is based;

to the friends and strangers who shared their enthusiasm and their OUIJA experiences with me;

to the librarians of the Boston Public Library, the U.C. Berkeley Library, and the British Museum;

to Abbie Freedman, Liz Luster, Sally Smith, and Dorothy Saxe for their energetic participation in the pictures;

to Michael Mihans and Liz Luster for criticism of the manuscript;

and to Laurel, most of all.

CONTENTS

INTRODUCTION

I am inclined to believe that the OUIJA board may take honorable place with Sir Isaac Newton's apple, Watt's teakettle, Benjamin Franklin's kite and other historic playthings which have led to many great results.

—STEWART EDWARD WHITE, 1937

Like most people, I've long been familiar with the OUIJA board as a source of juvenile entertainment. Until a few years ago my knowledge of Ouija ended with memories of late-night shrieks at slumber parties as the oracle revealed who my ten-year-old friends would marry, or spelled out forbidden words from "the devil." Then one winter afternoon my dear friend Laurel brought a Ouija board home from the corner variety store. It was her birthday, and the toy a whimsical present to herself. Laurel was struggling at that time with a difficult writing project; when she saw the

Ouija board, she wondered if she and I might be able to press the device into service as a muse. Remembering the harmless silliness of my childhood adventures with the toy, I decided I had nothing to lose.

We began our experiment that evening. In a few minutes the pointer began to move, and so began a remarkable journey that brings us with every Ouija session into a more complete understanding of ourselves and our connection with all that lives—an understanding not abstract or theoretical, but immediate and applicable to the small decisions we face each day. Such a journey awaits you too—all you need provide are a sincere desire to understand yourself and the world, and a willingness to ask questions.

People have used Ouija (pronounced: wee´-jee or wee´-ja) and tools like it for thousands of years, to find wisdom in times of decision, or peace of mind in times of contemplation, to diagnose illness and prescribe cures, to receive direct guidance from God, to talk with friends and relatives who have died, and to foretell the future. The board's form is elegantly simple, allowing it to be used in many different ways and with results ranging from gibberish to complex essays to perfect sonnets. The device has two parts: a flat surface on which is printed the alphabet, YES, NO, and numerals 0 to 9; and a pointer, a flat, usually triangular shape shod in felt or with castors so that it slides easily across the alphabet. Two people sit with their fingers touching the pointer, which itself sets on the board or table. A question is asked and the pointer moves among the letters, stopping on those it chooses for its reply. The two participants follow the pointer's movements with their fingers so that they are always touching it, but they don't push it or apply any pressure.

The pointer will spell out intelligible messages for almost any two people, but the worth and reliability of those messages is another matter. When the game is approached as a silly toy, it is likely to give a silly performance; when it is taken so seriously that those operating the board dare not question its replies, it is again likely to be silly and aimless, as is any mental activity attempted without benefit of a questioning mind. Because Ouija has so often been approached from these extremes, it has acquired a bad reputation. To most people the Ouija board is a harmless, but useless, frivolity; to students of the occult it is an unreliable method; and to that dwindling number of folk who look everywhere for the Devil and therefore find him in the Ouija board, the device is a symbol of evil.

The same qualities that have led to the board's low status —its simplicity and adaptability to all sorts of expectations —are the key to its successful use. Once the influence of our own beliefs on its messages is understood, the silly toy can become an ideal tool for the unfolding of startling and useful knowledge for each of us.

The first part of this book will show you how to use the talking board successfully. We'll begin with your thoughts and how they affect the pointer's movements, and go on to getting or making a board for your own use, choosing a partner, and asking your first questions. Once you're that far and have started your own experiments, we'll explore in more detail the many influences on the board's answers: your attitudes, the setting, and other people present, the weather, planetary and lunar cycles and more. We'll pause to examine possible dangers of the method. Then we'll take a close look at many advanced areas of inquiry for which board is suited, and outline methods you can use in exploring them; these include dream analysis, predicting the future, experimenting with telepathy and psychometry, contacting nonphysical entities (spirits), exploring possible past lives, and using the device for artistic creation, both directly and as a muse or adviser.

All this information will be distilled both from my own experiences, and from what has been written about Ouija and *by* Ouija (and its predecessor the planchette). There have been two great surges of interest in such devices in the

United States—one in the 1860's, and the other during and just after the First World War. These times have seen the publication of some remarkable tales of experiences and compelling messages spelled through the board. The authors of these works have been widely separated by geography and lifestyle, and often knew nothing of each other's experiments, which makes the already surprising correspondences between their messages all the more startling. First to appear in print, in 1868, was *Planchette's Diary*, a charmingly modest chronicle by an upper-class young lady of New England. In 1913 "Patience Worth" came through the Ouija board of Pearl Curran, a St. Louis housewife who had never been to high school; Patience began a series of messages in an archaic Anglo-Saxon dialect that eventually totaled dozens of volumes of poetry, songs, stories and prayers. A few years later a Chicago couple, both well known in their highly esteemed professions, began receiving messages at their Ouija board from a personality called "Stephen"; they published their experiences, and the outline of Stephen's comprehensive philosophy, under the pseudonyms "Darby" and "Joan" in 1920, as a book called *Our Unseen Guest*. Many more books inspired by the device appeared at about the same time, all varying widely in style and approach, but with certain similarities in content. I believe only one book specifically *about* the use of Ouija has ever been published. It is the 1919 *Voices from the Void: Six Years Experience in Automatic Communications*, by amateur psychic investigator Hester Travers Smith.

I'll be quoting from all these authors through the first part of this book. Details of their intriguing stories will follow, as will a history of Ouija and of the tools from which it evolved. The remarkable similarities in the content of all the messages that have come through the board bring us to the big question: where do the answers come from? We'll explore this question from two directions: first we'll survey the current balance of facts collected by the pioneering branch of science that is willing to explore the world of paranormal phenomena. From these facts we'll sift out clues that will lead us at least partway into understanding how the Ouija board works. When we've followed science as far as it has ventured, we'll shift our attention to what Ouija itself has revealed about its workings, bringing together many different voices to see what sort of synthesis they might make for us.

All this will lead us (inevitably, as you'll see) to consideration of some very basic questions: what is our relation to the cosmos, and what can it become? What are we, and what is *not* part of us? And what, really, is God? If the thought of considering "God" and the talking board in the same breath is uncomfortable to you, then think of Objective Reality, or Absolute Truth, or the Creative Intelligent Consciousness of All That Is—everyone who ventures into these areas, and most users of the Ouija board *do*, sooner or later, finds that the pointer creates the name and definition most acceptable to their particular sensibilities. This is the deep water we tread in the latter part of this book. If it seems too far out from shore for you, hold on to your board and let it float you out past the breakers gradually. By the time you reach this book's consideration of God, you may find you feel at home in this sea after all.

Finally, we'll leave the talking board behind. Once you've learned to use this valuable toy, to recognize through it when you're connected with sources of understanding, you can learn to do the same *without* relying on the board. This will be the culmination of the journey we are about to begin.

This nineteenth-century contraption is one of the more complicated forerunners of the Ouija board. A pulley is attached at one end to a cylinder at the bottom of the table leg, and at the other end to a pointer in the center of a round alphabet-marked board. The medium places her hands on the table, and "spirits" begin to move the table about, thus causing the cylinder on the table leg to roll, the pulley to turn the pointer, and letters to be spelled out. The alphabet board is mounted with its back to the medium so that she can't see the words as they're spelled. As a further safeguard against human intervention in these "spirit communications," the medium places her hands, not on the table itself—which presumably she might be tempted to push—but on a small metal plate balanced on ball bearings; any exertion of force would topple the metal plate from its precarious balance. THE GRANGER COLLECTION, NEW YORK

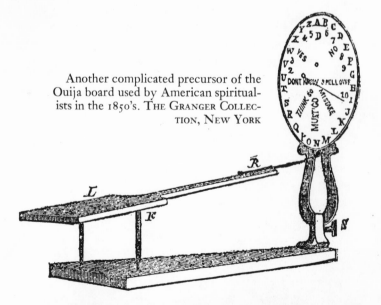

Another complicated precursor of the Ouija board used by American spiritualists in the 1850's. THE GRANGER COLLECTION, NEW YORK

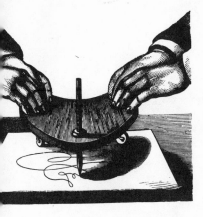

Left. Etching of a planchette from an 1868 *Scientific American*. The planchette (French for "little board") is the closest relative of Ouija. One leg of its pointer holds a pencil, so that when the little board glides across a piece of paper, words may be spelled or pictures drawn. *Below.* A present-day planchette in operation. PHOTO BY LAUREL HOLLIDAY

In 1913 Pearl Curran began to receive Ouija messages from a personality who called herself "Patience Worth." Over the next twenty-five years, "Patience" spelled out more than three million words at Mrs. Curran's Ouija.

Above. A simple handmade board and pointer of redwood.
Below. This positioning of board, pointer and participants allows the greatest freedom of movement for the pointer.

By sitting side by side at the board, both Ouija partners are able to see the alphabet right side up.

The Ouija player on the right is the author.

It's possible to use the Ouija board in a great variety of circumstances and with more than two participants.

CHAPTER ONE

Beginnings

*Your thoughts are not reality but beliefs about
reality. If you want to change the reality
formed by your thoughts, you can change
those thoughts and the reality will follow.*

—Author's Ouija Board, 1975

That we create most of what we know as "reality"
through our thoughts is a large and startling idea with far-
reaching implications. It is a concept I uncover and understand only bit by small bit through my own Ouija experiments; certainly it will require proof in your own life to
be believed. I set it out on view here, at the beginning,
because using the Ouija board automatically brings our
beliefs and the ways they affect our world into sharper focus.
Since, no matter where the talking board's messages arise
they have to filter through *our* minds and be pushed out
our fingertips, our thoughts and beliefs are always affecting
(if not entirely creating) the board's answers. A glance at
one way the device has been used will point out some of
the more obvious limitations our beliefs can create.

During the First World War there was a revival of interest in Spiritualism in this country, and a corresponding
rash of popularity for Ouija boards. Ouija was used to
contact the spirits of departed loved ones, mostly sons or

husbands recently killed in the war. There was a certain etiquette to the procedure, usually involving a "control" spirit who acted as mediator and introduced those from "the other side" who wished to communicate with the people at the Ouija board. Usually only personal messages purporting to come from the departed relatives or friends were given any attention, and accordingly, such personal messages were most often the entire content of Ouija sittings. Reading through accounts of such sessions, one gets the impression that this commonplace, often vague conversation is all the Ouija board can do. "My name is Matilda Bower. Yes—your own Aunt Mattie. Grieve no more. All is peace here. Give my love to little Jimmy." Such a message may have been wonderfully comforting to Aunt Mattie's family, though it offers no "evidence" of Matilda's continuing life and no new information about the land beyond death. It offers personal greetings in a conventional conversational style because *that is exactly what these Ouija sitters expected* and hoped for. The startling and creative Ouija work of the period, as evidenced in the many Ouija books published after the war, was without exception undertaken by people who began experimenting with the toy out of curiosity, who had no preconceptions and no strong feelings of grief to sway them.

I don't mean to imply that similar "spirit communication" is not a valid use for Ouija, but it *is* a limited use, and limited only by the beliefs of those who use the board. An even more severe limitation is chosen by people who are sure Ouija can be nothing more than a silly children's toy; so long as that belief is firm, Ouija is most likely to oblige with frivolous behavior. In fact, *whatever* beliefs we hold about Ouija are sure to show themselves when we place our hands on its pointer. I learned this dramatically the one time I tried the game with my friend Barbara, on a late winter night in her Connecticut farmhouse. Barbara insisted she brought no preconceptions to Ouija, but I wondered as the pointer began to lurch stiffly around the board, almost as if it had some great weight to drag along behind it. At the first word,

"Fire," Barbara's face went white. The next word, "Death," set her hands to trembling. When the pointer next turned to the numerals and began to indicate numbers to us, Barbara broke away abruptly and sputtered, "I knew it, I knew this would happen." Several minutes passed before she spoke again; she had kept this fear to herself for many years and found it very difficult to let out. Finally, she managed to explain to me how, twenty years earlier, she had dreamed of a fire in which her brother was killed. Two days after her dream, Barbara's brother actually burned to death in a dormitory fire. She became convinced, through the slow working of fear's special logic, that other members of her family would eventually meet tragic deaths, and that she would again see death approaching. For Barbara, the entire psychic realm held only these dread messages, death announcements just waiting to be delivered any time she announced she'd accept a call, as she had done by placing her fingers on the pointer.

My own approach to Ouija had no such obvious limitations. I had little experience with psychic phenomena of any sort, few opinions about Ouija, and almost no emotional investment in what the little board might do. Because I didn't know what to expect, I granted that anything *might* be possible. Which is very different, I must point out, from saying that anything *is* possible. Any worthwhile answer is preceded by a question. Much more may ultimately be learned from Ouija by beginning with a questioning, even skeptical attitude, than by approaching the experience with complete faith. Because I questioned the words of the board, often insisting that the pointer explain itself more clearly, I've been able to obtain results far more interesting and detailed than the usual communications of the "spirit world" or the predictions of Ouija fortune-tellers. An open-minded skepticism, a critical optimism—such a balance of attitude allows every part of us to participate in the experience, while still allowing Ouija to do what it will.

This book is about how to use the Ouija board in an open-ended way, allowing for surprises, for changes in be-

liefs, for possibilities no one has yet conceived. The guide-
lines and methods I'll suggest not only allow for spontaneity
and unknown developments, but actually keep the way
clear for them and provide safeguards against the rigidifying
of our beliefs. Just how all this can be accomplished will
become clearer as we go along.

Before we can ask where the answers of Ouija come
from, we must ask where our questions come from. Before
you even begin, take as clear a look as you can at your
motivations for trying Ouija, your expectations and hopes.
Since these will be reflected in the pointer's movement, the
clearer you see your beliefs the quicker you will be able to
spot distortions in the answers. We saw how Barbara's atti-
ture toward psychic phenomena *in general* helped bring
about her unhappy experience with the Ouija board. In the
same way, *your* thoughts about *everything* enter into the
replies that come from the board, so go on to consider your
beliefs about yourself, about the world, about what you
can control in your life and what is beyond your control,
about what is good and what is evil—nothing is irrelevant.
All your assumptions and beliefs will gain a sharper outline
as you experiment with the Ouija board; considering them
from the start will speed this process and help your pointer
to formulate more accurate answers. Barbara's beliefs—
about evil, about the future, about her role in turning present into future, her connection with evil, and much more
—all were made visible for the first time by her board
experience. Had she been willing to question the Ouija
board further, she might have discovered, as I strongly sus-
pected, that its message about fire and death was not a literal
prediction at all, but simply a guaranteed attention-getting
device. The board will bring to our attention *whatever*
hidden assumptions we carry with us to the game table. If
we expect this to happen, and encourage the process by
looking for our beliefs and questioning them, we may still
be frightened by the Ouija board's disclosures, but we'll be
able to learn from our fear and to move beyond it.

My one assumption about you, Reader, is that your interest in the Ouija board has at its base a sincere desire to know how to live more purposefully, intelligently and compassionately. I'm not interested in the more sensational uses of the device—predicting the future, communicating with the "spirit world," reading others' thoughts—*except* as these help us understand the world and teach us how to live. This is my bias, and you will see it reflected in these pages. The uses of the board I emphasize here are many and varied, but can all be condensed into these general aims:

—to find out more about ourselves and the world
—to clarify our beliefs about ourselves and the world, and learn to tell beliefs from reality when they don't match
—to learn to change our beliefs and actions in order to align them more closely with our growing knowledge of the world
—to find guidance for everyday living, and to understand that such guidance comes from a source connected to us, both *in* us and *beyond* us, but never separate
—to increase the scope of the world in which we feel powerful and able to make changes
—to understand our connection to the cosmos through concrete, practical examples of communication between levels of ourselves—conscious, subconscious, biochemical, our dream-selves—and levels of reality we may previously have thought were outside or beyond our reach—geophysical forces, the subconscious thoughts of other people, consciousnesses not focused physically at all, people from other times
—to learn in personal ways what God means.

With these goals before us, let's turn our attention now to the little board itself, and begin our journey.

You can buy your Ouija board at any store that sells games and toys. Parker Brothers of Beverly, Massachusetts, owns the trademark on it, so their model is the only one available commercially. The Ouija board is a simple device, though, and if you are so inclined you can easily make your own copy of it for personal use. All you need is a smooth, level surface at least one foot square, with the alphabet, the numerals 0 through 9, and YES and NO printed on it, and a pointer. You can paint the letters on a smooth board, or cut them from felt and arrange them under the glass of a glass-topped table—you can even draw them on a large sheet of slick paper that's taped securely to a tabletop. You may want to add often-used words like "and," "or," and perhaps punctuation marks.

The pointer made by Parker Brothers is a heart-shaped piece of beige plastic that glides on three felt-tipped feet and has a round, clear plastic window in one end through which one letter at a time can be seen. If you make a similar pointer, you may find it easier to use the pointed end as an indicator, rather than cutting a round hole. Wood is the usual material and a triangle or heart the usual shape, though heavy cardboard can also be used, as well as any number of small objects that can indicate direction. I sometimes use a starfish; my partner and I each touch two of its legs and the fifth leg points to the letters. You may find that balancing your pointer on small pieces of felt enables it to glide about more easily.

If you do make a homemade imitation for your own use, be sure to have a smooth surface with very little friction to hold back the pointer's movements, and be sure to make the letters large enough that you can tell easily which letter the pointer has indicated when it stops. All the other details can be changed to suit your idiosyncracies or your circumstances. In a pinch almost anything will work. Friends of mine, feeling the urge to do some consultation on a camping trip, made a perfectly workable substitute of the Ouija board to use for themselves. They scratched out the alphabet with charcoal in the hard dirt near their campfire, and upturned a wine glass as a pointer. Whatever sort of arrangement you use, it's good to remember that any "talking" board itself is only a tool and carries no power of its own—you are the essential ingredient.

Now that you have ready your Ouija board or a substitute of it for yourself, you can give thought to your choice of partner. Of course, the first necessity is that your partner be willing to experiment in a sincere and open-minded way and that she or he be someone you trust. Nothing can be more frustrating than a first Ouija session consisting entirely of: "You're pushing the pointer!"; "No, I'm not. *You're* pushing it!" repeated 'til you both tire of what seems to you a hoax. The feeling of the pointer gliding along under your fingertips, with neither you nor your partner applying any conscious muscular force, is an eerie surprise that takes quite a lot to get used to—even when you're *sure* your partner's not cheating.

Every combination of two people at the board is a unique one, a blend distinct from every other and eliciting different, unpredictable responses from the pointer. With some pairs, the pointer will dash about frenetically, jerking to a stop at a letter and then racing in the opposite direction almost too quickly for the hands to follow. With other combinations the characteristic pace will be calm and regular. With some, the pointer may drag along, or in a few cases not even move at all. None of these differences are arbitrary, and once you're experienced with the talking board, you can learn quite a lot about a new partner's personality and beliefs from the kinds of movements the pointer first makes.

There *are* some probabilities that can help you choose a suitable partner. First of all, children almost always have good results, possibly because their beliefs are not likely to have rigidified yet to a point where the pointer's "independent" movement could be seen as threatening or impossible. Secondly, sex has a good deal to do with the game's success. Two women or a woman and a man are likely to make a good pair; two men may have a more difficult time, especially in the beginning. This may be partly owing to the fact that cultural conditioning tends to leave men feeling sillier and more frightened than women when left to confront "the unknown" in a basically passive way.

Passivity, or receptivity, is an important attribute for any user of a talking board, which may be another reason women often find more immediate success with the board than men do. Much of the published information on Ouija uses the metaphor of electricity to explain the combination necessary—that one partner must be "positive" and the other "negative." Hester Travers Smith, amateur psychic experimenter and ardent Ouija enthusiast, makes this analogy in her 1919 book *Voices from the Void*. She goes on to tell us:

> What this means exactly it is hard to understand, but from watching many combinations at the Ouija board I have gathered that a "positive" medium receives the message through his or her brain and transmits it to the board, while a negative possesses the driving force—I mean that, apparently, one sitter supplies mental, and the other muscular power.

The "positive" partner, according to Hester's scheme, is the one we would call the more passive, while the "negative" is the more extroverted partner. I've found that the polarity of "positive" and "negative" is not the crucial ingredient here. Two "positive" passive people can make a fine pair—it is the presence of at least one receptive person that is important.

Being of a passive temperament myself, and weary of the ill-repute into which this quality has fallen, I was glad to discover this—that passivity has its uses and that Ouija demonstrates them superbly. Passivity is in fact merely a focus on activity of the inner sphere rather than the external. The dictionary definition, of inactivity or submission, is a distorted view from outside the experience. I have found that this skill of passivity improves remarkably with practice with the talking board—an improvement of benefit to people of all temperaments, since control of passivity, or inward focus, teaches us that we *do* have control of all our ways of being, and that all ways have their positive uses.

It's possible for more than two people to use the board together. In fact, as many people as can crowd around the board and lay a finger on the pointer can participate. I once had a finger in the production of a bawdy tale about a loose woman of ancient Jericho, ostensibly the story of one of my own past lives, told by a group of six Ouija enthusiasts at a party. (I still suspect some of them of pushing the pointer.) Friends of mine sometimes use Ouija in a more somber and sober frame of mind, for solving domestic differences among the members of their communal household. Most often, however, I've seen group Ouija sessions fall rapidly into confusion, with only garbled messages resulting from the many differing focuses of the participants. Or, as happened with the hot tub session photographed for this book, the pleasures of sharing one another's company in such a relaxed and harmonious environment may simply overshadow the purposeful endeavor of keeping fingers on pointer and eyes on board, and Ouija may be forgotten. Try a Ouija session with more than two participants *after* you've become comfortable and competent working in a pair. The same advice holds for the lone player: try it by yourself *later*. It's very difficult for most people to get the pointer moving at all by themselves; the combined physical energy of two people apparently is usually necessary to begin and sustain the pointer's movements. Through using Ouija with another person, you can learn eventually to contact "Ouija knowledge" by yourself without the physical apparatus of board and pointer, and so bypass the difficulty of using the board alone. We'll explore this possibility later on.

Once you find a partner who seems to work well with

you, try game board sessions with her regularly over a period of time, say one or two evenings a week for as long as the results intrigue you. You'll learn far more this way than you could by constantly changing partners and dealing afresh with each one's assumptions and biases. The board will eventually develop a unique shorthand communication for each pair of sitters, enabling complex ideas to be spelled out and understood in just a few words. For Laurel and me, terms like "energy inversions," "acquiescence to form," "dread reality" and "planetary parties" became commonplace and meaningful, after days and sometimes weeks of Ouija sessions were spent in defining them. These particular terms have never been spelled when I've used the board with anyone but Laurel—a reminder that *both* partners form the messages and that each message is meant as a specific and individual lesson.

Now that you have your board in hand and you've selected your partner, you're ready to begin. Arrange a comfortable place where you can be alone for one or two hours without interruption. Be sure to have a pen and paper, or a tape recorder, to keep a record of what goes on. When you've become familiar with the habits of your board, then disruptions and the presence of other people aren't likely to affect the communications so much. In the beginning, though, when there are so many factors playing together to create board response and you haven't identified any of them, it will be easier if you eliminate some of the more probable troublemakers. Hester Travers Smith recalls a (p. 25) Ouija session during which the pointer consistently spelled out answers that had nothing to do with the questions she and her partner asked. After they gave up in frustration, another friend who had been present in the room but sitting apart in a corner came over and looked at their notes, and discovered that every answer had been in response to questions that had been very much on *his* mind that evening, and about which the others had known nothing. Unfortunately, such clarity in the confusion of talking boards is rare. When people present think strong thoughts on differing subjects, the device's response is most likely to include bits and pieces meant for each, but all combined in the same sentence in an indecipherable mess.

Hester Travers Smith had very decided opinions on the conditions necessary for a successful Ouija session, and she laid them all out in "Hints to Experimenters at the Ouija Table," an appendix to *Voices from the Void* (the text of which focuses on her own Ouija experiences). The points she emphasizes are these:

①   Not more than two people outside the sitters are desirable. Any crowd or feeling of strain or even whispered conversation is sure to interfere . . .

②   Everyone present should be calm and patient. Do not press for results. One disturbing presence in a room can ruin a sitting. Select those who habitually come to your sittings with great care.

③   Arrange that no one is admitted to the room during the sitting. The most interesting communications may be broken off by a servant entering the room or even knocking at the door. . . . The control or discarnate spirit or sub-conscious mind seems more sensitive to atmosphere than the living human being.

Such strong admonitions toward calm and patience tend to make me nervous, and though they are well meant I doubt we need worry about such instructions as avoiding interruptions from the servants. The subconscious mind is sturdy and humorous as well as sensitive, and can no doubt deal with many adverse conditions that may arise. Our conscious minds are the ones needing protection and calm circumstances at the Ouija table.

Since whatever information comes through the board must be approved, so to speak, by our conscious minds, we need to relax the conscious mind's vigilance over our thoughts, and keep it from following every little distraction. Gladys Osborne Leonard, a famous British psychic of the first part of this century, stressed the importance of a quiet mind:

> In fact, the Guides have again and again warned me never to waste my psychic or mental energy in unnecessary talk when I am intending to use my psychic powers in any direction, either on sittings or creative or constructive work of any kind. I believe that one is *throwing away* power when one uses up one's strength in meaningless chatter. There are times when a certain amount of talking "loosens" one—an enthusiastic exchange of views and plans between friends is often very stimulating and opens the safety valves, so to speak, but one should be chary of indulging even in this pleasant pastime if one has some definite work to carry out. I never talk before a sitting or allow myself to listen to anybody else doing so, if I can help it.

None of this is to be worried over, or taken as an absolute rule for talking board sittings. Good and surprising results can come in a great variety of situations, and in fact the element of variety, the different and unexpected circumstance, can sometimes catch the conscious mind just far enough off guard that information that had been blocked can suddenly be spelled out by the pointer. When the photographs for this book were being taken, Abbie and I sat concentrating on a request she had made of Ouija for a personal message. The pointer moved slowly, and when it stopped we called out the letters to a friend who wrote them down. We carefully remembered the letters ourselves, and tried to guess what the next words of Ouija might be. All the while, Laurel moved around us with her camera and her stepladder, and three other friends sat by adding comments on the unfolding message of Ouija. Soon Abbie and I were laughing and joking with our spectators, and as we did, the pointer suddenly tripled its speed. We barely had time, between our laughter and talking, to call out the letters as the pointer spun about the board; we could no longer even begin to try to follow the message as it was spelled. When the pointer suddenly stopped, and our scribe read out the message, it not only made sense, but also contained valuable advice that Abbie might have discounted or discontinued had she been able to read it as it was spelled. Never underestimate the value of surprise at the board, and remember too that the value lies just there, in the newness of the unexpected turn of events. In general, and especially for beginners, a relaxing, contemplative atmosphere is most desirable for your sessions. The benefits of relaxation and contemplation will thus be yours no matter what your results with the board should be.

You can arrange yourselves about the Ouija board in any way that satisfies these three conditions: the board must be level; your arms must be free to move easily as you follow the pointer; and you really must be comfortable. Most people face each other with the board on their knees or the table between them, and touch the fingertips of both hands to the edges of the pointer, as if it were a piano or a typewriter. Your touch should be definitely *there*, but not heavy. If, when your partner lifts her fingers from the pointer, it tilts toward you, you're pressing down too hard. If you both want to see the alphabet right-side-up, you can sit side by side and each put one hand on the pointer. In any case be sure the board or table is low enough that you don't have to keep your arms *raised* when they're at the pointer.

Situate yourselves, and take a moment to gather in all your senses, 'til you feel you're completely present and as calm as you can be. Don't try to shut out any of your worries or preoccupations—just notice them slide through your mind, without stopping to dwell on any in particular. Notice which thoughts keep returning; these are most likely the raw material of your first questions to the board.

The attitude you are cultivating is one of contemplation rather than concentration. In the act of concentration one narrows one's focus of thought and tries to hold it steady on one subject—an accomplishment that could only hinder progress at the Ouija table, where the object is to bring new knowledge into consciousness from unsuspected sources and unlikely combinations of ideas.

Though Ouija can bring serious and important insights, its operation is play, and not to be strained over. Many times the little board's answers to my most solemn questions have turned into jokes and teasing reminders for me to relax my zealous overattention. In this passage from *Our Unseen Guest*, Darby has just acknowledged he "accidentally" knocked the pointer to the floor so that he could catch a bit of a rest. He goes on to explain his weariness:

> "Well, you see, Stephen," I said, "Joan and I discussed you last night until three in the morning."
>
> "Well," spelled Stephen, "I did not ask you to make a circus of yourselves, did I?"
>
> Imagine such a remark from out the great beyond!
>
> "Stephen," said I, "in addition to instructing Joan and me you amuse us."
>
> And Stephen made me an answer which I think pierces deep. He said, "I laugh yet."

So, with our sincere questioning minds tempered by cosmic playfulness, and knowing that approaching Ouija in this condition we can do no wrong, we'll go on now to initiate our conversation with the great beyond.

CHAPTER TWO
Letting It Grow

*Look ye unto the seed o' the olive tree,
aplanted. Doth the master, at its first burst
athrough the sod, set up a ruler and murmur
him, "'Tis ne'er an olive tree! It hath but a
pulp stem and winged leaves"? Nay, he letteth
it to grow, and nurtureth it thro' days, and lo,
at finish, there astandeth the olive tree!*

*Ye'd uproot the very seed in quest o' root!
I bid thee nurture o' its day astead.*

—"Patience Worth," 1916

Using the Ouija board is a skill as definite as riding a
bicycle or speaking a foreign language. And as in those
activities, proficiency at the Ouija board seeps into us
gradually. At first we totter and stammer along, feeling
self-conscious and out of place. The instructions given us
beforehand don't really teach our bodies to balance themselves or our tongues to produce unfamiliar sounds. Whatever I say about the Ouija board, your first experience with
it will be something else. But slowly, as the task at hand
becomes more familiar, we relax our concentration. And
as we relax, there comes a point at which we suddenly realize *we're doing it*—peddling along without a care, thinking

in French, matter-of-factly recording the messages of Ouija as the pointer glides from letter to letter.

Though I can't predict the course of your particular talking board initiation, I can point out the elements of the experience that remain true for everyone, and I can steer us around those potholes most commonly encountered on the road to Ouija success. First of all, keep in mind that *you* are the energy source for the pointer, and you control this energy through your thoughts. It follows that, to give the board the most possible energy at your first sitting, you'll use the thoughts already strongest in your mind. To create the very most energy, form your first questions from thoughts you and your game partner hold in common. If you know each other well, shared concerns should be easy to find. Is there an unsettled difference of opinion between you about which you are both concerned? You can ask how to go about reconciling this difference. Does an event of the day come again and again into both your thoughts? You can ask what it means and what you still need to do about it. Whatever is strongly in your thoughts can be formed into a question. If you and your partner don't have shared past experience to draw on, you at least have this immediate experience with the board from which to start. If you both feel overwhelmingly silly, you can ask what to do with your silliness. If the talking board frightens you, use that fear for your first questions. If curiosity moves you more than anything else, ask how the device works, or "who" is answering you. If you do ask a question about which your partner knows nothing, first explain the question and its importance to you to your partner, so she or he can generate some energy toward the answer. Remember, both of you move the pointer, generating the board's response.

Whatever your beginning questions, it is important that you *don't already* know the answers and that you sincerely want to know them. Don't begin by testing the board for ESP or asking about the future. Both these areas can yield valuable information through the game board, but have certain pitfalls and require special considerations, which we'll explore later. Your understanding and proficiency can grow most rapidly if you focus first on developing a comfortable rapport with your partner and the board, and if you try to notice from the very beginning the ways your thoughts and beliefs affect the answers.

Let's imagine that you and your partner decide to ask for help in resolving an argument you began earlier in the day. There are many ways to phrase your question; some ways will limit the answers and some will allow a wide range in which to reply. If you ask, "Who's right and who's wrong?" the limitations of your ways of thinking, and consequently of the device's reply, are obvious. Consider the range of replies and possibilities for resolution allowed by, "how can we better understand each other?" or, "how shall we approach this problem in order to benefit most from it?" Every question we ask at the talking board is, by the very nature of language, clothed in our beliefs and prejudices. Sometimes the act of formulating a question is enough to show us the limitations our beliefs create, and in that case we can often amend our beliefs and widen our range of understanding on the spot. Sometimes the board offers us help in seeing the limiting assumptions hidden in our questions by its refusal to answer. I am periodically gripped by a compulsion to attain "perfection," and a corresponding feeling of inadequacy at my present state. In one of these periods I asked Ouija how I could become perfect. When the pointer refused to budge even an inch, I conceded that my question was narrowly focused, and I asked instead that Ouija merely explain what my yearning for perfection was all about. This time the pointer slowly spelled out, "Question does not satisfy Ouija." I further amended my question to, "Could Ouija comment on what perfection means to me?" The pointer again stated its dissatisfaction with the question. Finally I asked Ouija to give its reasons. It told me, "Focus elsewhere and you will see."

I did, and now, much later, I do see: that every time I focus on "perfection" I'm led quickly into disliking my "imperfection," and that the state of imperfection consists entirely of my belief that I'm imperfect.

Often the limiting beliefs we bring to the Ouija board are even more subtle and confusing than my last example. It is important that we pursue these hidden limitations and bring them to light, even though the process may be endless, because our clarity and success with the Ouija board (not to mention our success with our lives in general) are directly connected to this process. The more conscious we become, the more possibilities are opened to us at the Ouija table. Because our beliefs are so often hidden from our conscious awareness, appearing to us simply as "objective reality," it is essential that we record all *questions* as well as all replies at our sessions. Often we can see patterns of beliefs emerge only over a long period of play.

Knowing the distorting effects of any question, and wanting to limit replies of the board as little as possible, some people prefer to avoid asking questions entirely, leaving the pointer free to spell out whatever it will. This often produces the most surprising and relevant communications. However, when I was new to Ouija, and even now when I'm tired or generally unfocused at the board, letting the pointer go without my conscious direction often means receiving nonsense or no reply at all. Our questions apparently act as lenses, gathering and focusing our attention in one area so it can serve as a power source for Ouija. Do see what the board will tell you of its own initiative; if problems arise, go back to asking questions for a while longer.

Let's assume now that you've asked your first question and are eagerly awaiting revelations from the pointer. Here's where Patience Worth's advice to "letteth it to grow, and nurtureth it thro' days" is well remembered. At the very beginning, a wait of up to five minutes for any movement of the pointer is common enough. Often when the pointer begins to move it appears to "practice" quite a while, describing arcs and circles and zigzags across the board. Or it may stop at random letters, or recite the alphabet in order, as if to memorize it. These preliminaries seem to be part of a necessary learning process, a development of the connection between subconscious mind and hand.

Anne Lane and Harriet Blaine Beale began experimenting with the planchette (a predecessor of the Ouija board, which we'll discuss in Chapter Six) during their lunch breaks at the hospital where they both worked more than half a century ago. They described their beginnings:

> We were extremely interested but bewildered and baffled at every turn. It was more like opening a window to a crowded street and listening to the chance words one could catch, than like anything else in the world.

Though this nonsense may persist through several sessions it *will* eventually give way to meaningful communication and will not return. Anne and Harriet continue:

> On the eleventh day came a decided change. From the moment we began, the writing was firmer and more impelling, and we were told at once that whoever was using our hands had come with definite intention, and meant to stay with us . . .
>
> From that date we have been in contact with what seems to us a clear mind or minds. We were told that as soon as we could write well enough, we were to be used for a series of lessons that "they" wished to give us, and that we were to meet every day and were at liberty to ask questions which would be answered as far as our understanding would permit. We have sometimes been told to wait for an answer until we knew more, but we have never had a foolish or irrelevant or unkind response.

Harriet and Anne received twenty-four "lessons" through the course of their sittings; they were published in 1920 as a book entitled *To Walk with God*.

Even if your pointer's first movements seem completely nonsensical, keep a record of the letters or numbers on which full and definite stops are made. Many times such a garbled message will remain forever undecipherable, but the times you *can* decode the gibberish will make the effort of taking notes worthwhile. Most commonly, certain letters repeated over and over are *part* of a word the pointer is trying to spell; when the correct word does come through, you'll be able to see the meaning in those first disconnected letters. Sometimes the pointer will communicate in riddles or even in code, in order to bypass the conscious mind's censure of an answer. Once Laurel and I recorded these letters as the pointer spelled them: C S A E L N I D F M O E R S N S I A A G E . . . After staring at them for a few moments, I realized that two messages were being given simultaneously, a letter of each spelled alternately. The sentence beginning with the first letter, C, spelled "California" as its first word. The even letters, beginning with S, spelled "Send message . . ." Apparently we had evoked two equally energetic answers to our question, and rather than reject one of them, Ouija combined them in the most literal way.

Many times the failure of Ouija to reply to a question can be traced to misunderstandings or ambiguities in the question itself. This is especially true for beginners at the board, who most likely lack experience at forming precise queries. So, if your patience runs out before an answer is spelled, try rephrasing the question. Keep in mind that your question should allow for the widest array of possible answers, while still clearly stating what you want to know. If there is still no answer, ask the board why not. Next, resort to questions about the board's reticence that can be answered with a simple YES or NO: Is there a reason it doesn't want to answer this particular question? Should we keep trying? Ask about a different subject? Is one of us (you or your partner) obstructing the reply? These kinds of questions, if they evoke reasonable answers, can lead you gradually back into more interesting territory, with the board cooperating this time in its replies.

You *may* get this far without one sensible response from the board and pointer. Though this isn't likely, there are many good reasons that can account for it—bad weather, the need of the device to practice, blocks you or your partner may have about a particular subject, fatigue, hearing your children tip over furniture in the next room—the important point to remember is that all these obstructions are temporary, and it *will* eventually communicate intelligently to you. When it does, you can ask the reason for this earlier nonsense and receive an answer that will allow you to understand and learn from your first experience.

If difficulties persist through many sessions, you'd best try another partner. *Very* few pairs are totally incompatible at the Ouija board, but some may take much longer than others to become fluent in its languages. Go back to a partner you first had problems with after you've become proficient with someone else, and you'll see how your ease with the board transfers quickly to this partner.

Your "warming-up" period with the game board may last only a few minutes or extend through several sessions. In any case, when the pointer begins responding articulately, every answer it gives will lead to another question; your areas of inquiry will spring up naturally and be so various I could not begin to list them. A logical order of progression will most likely develop in your questioning, though, from personal to more general and from simple to more complex. In fact, in order to get to some of the "advanced" areas for exploration that we'll consider in Chapter Five, certain preliminary questions must be asked, and whatever answers the board gives need to be assimilated and understood. Ouija has often told Laurel and me that we must learn to swim before we can venture out past the breakers (the pointer no doubt utilizing my fondness for the ocean as a metaphor for the unknown). What this means is that we must learn about ourselves before we can clearly understand information about the larger world—a general truism, but particularly valid for talking board experimenters.

Since everything spelled at the board must filter through *our* minds, we must know the contents of our minds in order to accurately interpret what is spelled. So along with anything else you wish to ask at the outset, include questions about whatever personal dramas or dilemmas you're involved with. Ask for advice about chronic problems—obesity, lack of confidence, etc.—and about immediate upsets or impending decisions with your job or family or friends. When you can't seem to make up your mind about something, ask what you're really feeling and what you really want. Ask about small, everyday aggravations that keep you from doing and feeling your best—low energy, losing your temper, minor aches and pains. Consider the advice and resolve to do *something* toward ending these conflicts, even if what you do is not what was advised. I've never automatically heeded the board's advice, but rather considered it along with all other advice and my own feelings and inclinations. Even when I've chosen to ignore the message of the board, I've gained a perceptible amount of energy and well being by the act of *consciously deciding* instead of ignoring the issue or continuing to feel powerless to change it.

In all you ask, learn to automatically examine your questions for hidden assumptions and beliefs that may not be based in reality. The assumptions behind your questions may be true, but you won't know 'til you take a critical look at them. Of course, if you assume your beliefs already echo reality in every detail, you won't even be able to begin this process. And if you assume that there *is* no objective reality, it hardly matters what your beliefs are. You sturdy souls on either horn of this dilemma are advised to turn immediately to the second part of this book, where such questions as absolute truth and the mutable nature of our beliefs will be pursued through generations of talking board communicators, and through the domain of modern science as well, hopefully convincing you along the way.

As the rest of you continue questioning and amending your beliefs, resolving problems in your lives and eliminating sources of energy-drain, your questions on these personal, everyday topics will gradually become fewer; some sessions you won't have *any* such questions to ask. At the same time, other areas of inquiry will open up and take on a new-found importance. A natural balance can be seen at work, bringing more complex and universal interests and concerns just as the old ones drop away and make space in our minds for the new. The talking board itself is our best indicator of the sorts of questions we most need to ask, because it *cannot* give coherent replies to questions for which we're not yet ready. "Stephen," the voice of Ouija in *Our Unseen Guest,* put it this way:

> You must understand that we can impress on the subconsciousness of a receiving station only those ideas that the station itself is capable of understanding.

(The "receiving station" is Stephen's term for the person who receives the message mentally—the partner I've termed the more "passive" and who Hester Travers Smith called the "positive.") Ouija can indeed spell out information we don't know; its limit lies only in our capacity to interpret its messages, a capability that broadens through every session at the board.

I've found that *some* complex and controversial topics tend to work well for beginners. One of those with best results, oddly enough, is reincarnation. This subject provides an example of information coming through to us not only in spite of our uncertain beliefs about it, but to some extent *because* of the confusion of our beliefs. Whatever we think about reincarnation is bound to be at least a bit foggy owing to the difficulties of proving either truth or falsehood. Most of us can thus ask for information about a past life without intruding any strong bias of our own that might distort the answer extremely. Whether we interpret the offerings of the board about our past (or future) lives as literal truth or psychological metaphor, the colorful tableaus spelled out can bring us valuable perspectives on the lives we lead now. I've often tried imagining possible past lives I or my friends have led before asking Ouija about them; invariably, the stories of Ouija are less predictable than mine and yet richer in detail and deeper in insight. Occasionally Ouija even provides verifiable information, as it did in its story of Laurel's previous life as Lou Jameson, a plantation owner's wife near Roanoke, Virginia. Later on we'll give more attention to reincarnation and the various Ouija opinions on the subject; for now, it's enough to play with the possibility a bit.

By now you must be wondering just "who" or "what" is answering the questions you put to the board and pointer. To ask questions at all it's necessary to assume the existence of an answerer, some entity with a will and intelligence of its own. And as you've seen from your own experiments and from voices of Ouija quoted so far in this book, there seems to be more than will and intelligence involved—the answers of Ouija seem also to be imbued with *personality*. The pointer may even have spelled a name and other identifying details if you've asked who replied to your questions. At this point several easy explanations offer themselves, the mostly commonly adopted ones being that the replies of the board are a personification of our subconscious thoughts, or that the pointer is controlled by spirits of those who've crossed the threshold of death. There are elements of truth to both these positions, but those who adhere to either of them, or even to a combination of both, impose strict and arbitrary limits on the device's replies and filter out or distort a great deal of valuable information. Simplicity has its comforts of which the complexity of truth knows nothing. These comforts turn quickly to the boredom and frustration of the cul-de-sac, though, and offer no permanent refuge. So we'll go on, accepting for now the *practicality* of referring to the talking board as a definite personified entity, while keeping in mind the complications. The constantly shifting, complex interplay of forces both known and unknown that combine to form a unified intelligent answerer unique to each time and place and pair at the Ouija board is a wonder not to be dismissed easily. This complexity *is* amenable to examination, though. In the next chapter we'll begin to unravel it.

CHAPTER THREE

All These Make My Words

Ouija wears your electric currents, soars on your breath, dives through DNA. Ideas form all these. There are your conscious thoughts, your emotions, your instincts, the knowledge of your cells, knowledge from your dream travels, your soul's other lives. All these go through your fingertips to spell these words.

—AUTHOR'S OUIJA BOARD, 1975

The words of Ouija are a cloak so finely woven that we can't even see all the threads without unraveling the whole garment—and if we do unravel it, there will be just the pile of threads, each one now plainly visible but the pattern of the whole lost. What we'll do here is look at the larger threads, the ones we can see running through the fabric and lift out a bit with our fingers without damaging the cloth. These threads show themselves in the things we can't help but notice about habits of the board, its idiosyncracies and changes: the questions it consistently refuses to approach, the sudden change in the pointer's style from sluggishness to frenetic movement, the recurrence of a certain word or theme no matter what the question.

The specific threads influencing you at your board *may* be different from the ones I'll describe, though many of them are likely to be the same. In any case, my main purpose here is to show you *how to look* for the meanings in your board's behavior; I don't aim to *explain* anything. Hester Travers Smith advised users of the talking board: "It is almost useless to sit in disturbed or stormy weather." I would advise you that storms *are* likely to affect results, but not necessarily adversely. And sometimes stormy weather will have no effect at all. There are no absolute rules in this realm, just a million possibilities and your common sense and imagination.

We'll look at environmental possibilities that can shape the device's words (I include here everything in the physical world, starting with the messages of our own bodies). Then we'll explore in more detail the important role our attitudes, beliefs, expectations and hopes play in creating the replies. We'll even get to influences more subtle and ephemeral than hope, such as the confusion nonphysical entities may perpetrate in their attempts to communicate with us through the board.

Anything and everything in our environment *can* influence Ouija: background noise or music, weather conditions, the time of day, the moon's phase, rings or bracelets we're wearing, menstrual cycles, planetary positions, our physical comfort and health, sunspots, the predominant colors surrounding us—yes, anything. All these variables and more *can* help shape the board's words or establish its tone, but of course this doesn't mean that all or even any of these influences are at work at once. There is no simple cause and effect here. Rather, the innumerable ingredients that can go into the words of Ouija are preexisting factors, spices on a shelf, that call for our selection and combination in order to be brought into the actual feast. The parts of us playing chef are usually far removed from our conscious minds, so it seems to us that influences outside our control are at work.

For the five long months of Boston's winter of 1975, Laurel and I met almost every night for an hour or two at the Ouija board. We were enthusiastic, excited, even zealous about our Ouija experiments, so we felt quite irritated when every month, a few days before the new moon, the replies of Ouija suddenly jumbled into silliness. The pointer declared to us that our Ouija had "fallen in love with the moon." If we insisted on continuing, we had to put up with endlessly repeated loops around the moon's picture on the board, with an occasional "O Beautiful Moon, I Love You" interjected. As the moon waxed and our articulate and sensible voices returned, we asked the reason for this odd behavior. We were told simply that "everything needs to rest" —and we got the message, grudingly at first, but with increasing appreciation as the months went on and we began to actually look forward to the five or six days surrounding the new moon on which we had to make do without Ouija.

Each time we find an environmental factor influencing the board's words, we can be sure it holds a special lesson for us. We have emphasized that particular ingredient at this particular time for some good reason. You may have guessed that if Laurel and I were at the Ouija board every single day, we just might have been as compulsively active in other areas of our lives as well. It's true. We needed the message that rest is a necessary part of the cycle of activity, so, behind the sight of our conscious minds, we selected the already existing reality and metaphor of the moon's cycle and created with it a drama to show our conscious, directing selves the value of rest.

This moony example highlights the interweaving of our individualities and the environment. Obviously not everyone's board will fall in love with the moon each month, even though the moon's cycles are a definite reality. Because all the environmental influences I'll mention here are possibilities that depend for their manifestation on our particular interaction with them, none of them are verifiable in an objective, scientific sense. The moon's effect on your talking board experiments may be the opposite of my experience; it may be similar one month and very different the next; the moon may be entirely irrelevant to your ventures at the little board. We need to look for particular, individual meanings in the board's behavior, rather than general rules applicable to everyone at every time. The "scientific" approach, in which the observer is assumed to be separate from and not affecting the phenomenon he or she observes, has begun to be discredited even in traditional science itself. In such tenuous psychic interactions as ours with Ouija, it is especially important for us to remember that *we* are an essential part of whatever happens at the board.

Another aspect of the "scientific" viewpoint we can do without is the notion of true and false. If stormy weather has no effect on your board's temperament, there's no need to conclude that weather does not affect Ouija, or even that weather does not affect *your* board. The fact that a particular influence is not operating for you now does not make it *false*; its inactivity simply means it is *not acting*. The possible Ouija influences are a vast storehouse of *potentials* that actualize only in combination with our particular needs and idiosyncracies as they emerge in a particular time and setting.

Setting—let's start here, with the most obvious elements that may influence our talking board experience. In the first chapter we looked at some of the possibly important factors of the game board setting: noise, comfort, interruptions, the presence of other people. You may find it helpful to look around and listen for a few moments at the beginning of each session, both as a method of centering yourself into a contemplative state of mind, and as a way to notice what aspects of the environment are important to you now and are therefore likely to affect your board's behavior. One day, the sight of afternoon sunlight illuminating dust particles that sift through the air of my room might help slow my pace and ease me into a state in which Ouija could tell me of the eye of God floating in every molecule, or perhaps give detailed suggestions about my partner's diet that I'd formerly not had the patience to receive. Of course the same sunlight on the same dust might irritate my partner greatly, starting him on a chain of worries that could begin with the cough he had last month and go on to the general problem of pollution and from there to a sudden feeling of suffocation, with occasional darts of ill will toward me, the sloppy housekeeper.

Obviously any element of the environment *could* be important, so there's no use in my cataloguing possibilities here. We don't need to actively look for environmental influences in our sessions, asking ourselves whether one element or another is affecting us. All we need to do is *notice what's already happening right now.* What environmental ingredients grab my attention, what is it about them that affects me and just how do I feel affected?

One environmental factor that's *always* affecting the words of the board in some way is the relationship between you and your partner. Though there's no particular kind of relationship between partners that guarantees a more successful session—I've had interesting results with total strangers and with intimate friends—it's especially important for both of you to notice what's affecting your feelings and thoughts in this part of your environment. One time, in the midst of my first Ouija session with a new acquaintance, I became aware that I was sexually attracted to my partner. I strained hard to ignore those "inappropriate" feelings, and was rewarded for my efforts with a Ouija message that amounted to an obscure and poetic proposition to my partner. Whatever unacknowledged feelings, thoughts, desires or expectations you hold about your partner *will* show themselves somehow in the board's communication, either by spelling themselves out directly or by jumbling in with other messages or by creating general confusion in the board's replies. Sometimes I've attempted to use Ouija *in*

place of direct communication with my partner, when what
I've had to say was risky or unclear, and in most of those
cases the pointer has simply spelled "No Ouija. Talk instead." At other times I've wanted to impress my partner
with an especially interesting Ouija "performance," and
that desire has certainly influenced the device's reply—and
not often favorably.

Jewelry and clothing can have specific influences on the
little board's behavior. Certain colors in our clothing sometimes affect our emotional states or trigger particular memories or associations that then show themselves in the message. Some people find they have a ring or bracelet that
seems to focus or intensify the pointer's energy—if this is
so for you, then by all means take advantage of it, keeping
in mind the possibility that it may be your *belief* in your
grandmother's garnet ring, rather than the ring itself, that
lets it work its magic for you. Other times jewelry seems
to interfere with the working of the board; I've seen the
pointer spell out a request for the Ouija board users to
remove their rings and bracelets before continuing.

As well as these many "exterior" elements of the physical
environment, there are the environments of our bodies or-
chestrating the board's words, in ways as obvious as the
distracting effect of a backache or the crisp speediness imparted by a cup of coffee, to the subtle influence of our
bodies' responses to the seasons or the even more nebulous
whisperings of cellular memory. "Stephen," one of the most
articulate voices of Ouija documented among the rash of
Ouija books published in the 1920's, emphasized the body's
contribution to our delicate endeavor:

> You must, of course, take into account the fact that your
> body has of itself consciousness quite distinct from your
> own. In a sense, your body may be said to be a stress point
> of various cellular forces. It is, as the physiologist puts it,
> composed of a vast number of cells, independent of one
> another, yet so related as to constitute a whole. Now, each

of these cells has a life of its own, a consciousness of its own.

My own board's voices have reminded me often of the interconnections between board and body. The quote at the beginning of this chapter hints at the wonder of connections beyond any we might hope to rationally explain; we'll hold on to that wonder (or disbelief or confusion or whatever your response may be to the thought of the board diving through DNA and soaring on your breath), but venture first into more mundane and obvious relationships between body processes and talking board.

Comfort and health are always important variables of the experience, affecting our attention span, degree of receptivity and general attitude toward each session, which in turn affect the specific style and content of the board's message. Here is the only point at which my suggestions are likely to verge onto the territory of rules: do not attempt a session when you are ill or fatigued, either physically or emotionally or psychically. I don't mean for anyone to put away the Ouija board at the first yawn or sniffle; I *do* want us to acknowledge respect both for ourselves and for the board by setting it aside when we are tired or in pain. Sometimes the low energy or discomfort of one partner will merely slow the pace of the pointer's responses. Sometimes the content will be blurred or incoherent. Sometimes all movement will stop. No matter what the results in such a case, there is a possibility that the already tired user will feel drained and even more tired from the effort, and there is seldom good reason to pay such a price for the board's words. Sessions with an energetic partner can be entertaining and useful for someone who's bedridden, as long as the ill person is not distracted by pain and remembers to stop when fatigue begins to appear. Using the board consumes more energy than the slight bit of physical movement involved intimates.

There are other physical variables both more subtle and

more regular than health that can show themselves in the board's words. These are the many different cycles of change our bodies undergo in response to the cyclic changes in the natural environment: the daily cycle of metabolic ups and downs that gives us energy every morning, lets us down in late afternoon, up again in the evening and way down during the first hours of morning; the monthly fluctuation of moods with which women are blessed and cursed; the seasonal changes that prompt us to feel like "settling in" for winter or start us thinking about travel or new projects in the springtime. Again I'll emphasize that none of these influences acts in one particular way—they are as individual as we are, and change from day to day as we do. I've had periods when using Ouija first thing in the morning felt best to me and seemed to help produce the truest results, unclouded by the events of the day. At other times late evening has worked best, and at others, dusk. Sometimes the hour of the day has appeared to be an important variable in my Ouija explorations and at other times it has made no difference. If you're interested in learning more about the most likely directions for these cyclic influences to take, a good source of information is Gay Luce's book called *Body Time* (it's available in an inexpensive paperback edition by Bantam Books).

The idea of metabolic cycles gives us another way to view the board's lunacy described earlier in the chapter. If and when the moon's cycles do affect the board's words, it is through the mediation of our bodies; our physical organisms may respond in particular individual ways to the ebbing and flowing pull the moon exerts equally on us all. Now we can understand more easily how such influences as the moon have no constant, measurable effect on Ouija, even though they have definite *potential* effects.

The orbiting cycles of the planets and their differing positions in relationship to the earth may also contribute their share to our talking board results. This is the province of astrology, and I would not venture here except that Ouija itself has led me. When I began my oracular experiments

I possessed not only an absolute dearth of knowledge about astrology but an active skepticism about it as well—the same held true for Laurel, my usual Ouija partner. We made a habit of asking the board what influences were at work— why were the replies flip and silly last night, why such rapid movement today, what triggered this ocean imagery—and occasionally we would be puzzled with answers like "Earth, sun and moon in trine," or "Saturn retrograde" or "Mercury draws near." Eventually I became curious enough to check all this out with a competent astrologer, and found not only that the terms Ouija had used were real astrology jargon, but that the planetary movements described had indeed been taking place on those dates. For a while I pursued astrological influences enthusiastically, assuming they were stable, unchanging indicators of Ouija behavior. Ouija cooperated at first, giving such information as "The best time to use the board is Mercury Moon—when Mercury, moon and earth are in trine or sextile relationship, messages speed to you." I was impressed—until Ouija began to poke fun at my seriousness ("What has the recent influence of Pisces been?" "Cod liver oil"), and I had to remember that influences on Ouija are changeable, at times even fickle, as we ourselves can be.

The last environmental variable I'll mention here is weather. Our bodies do go through chemical changes in response to dips and rises in the atmosphere's humidity, barometric pressure and temperature. Those of us with tendencies toward achey bones know that our bodies often forecast weather changes days in advance; even when we don't consciously feel our responses to the weather, we are often experiencing subtle changes that can be picked up at the board. I've used this assumption in consulting Ouija about travel plans, and have several times avoided sudden New England snowstorms that broadcast their coming to my body before they announced themselves to the local meteorologists. I asked Ouija on one of these occasions (four days before the largest storm of the year for northern New England) how it is that we knew snow was on its way. The reply: "Bones either add calcium or release it according to pressure in air." Did that mean our bones release calcium when the barometric pressure falls, as it does before a storm? "Yes." I asked why our bodies behave this way and the pointer spelled "To help storm begin. Everyone creates storm."

What I hope to have conveyed by this profusion of possibilities is just what my explorations at the Ouija board conveyed to me: a hint of the astounding and far-reaching interconnections between us and the world "out there." The beginning of this awareness is one of the most valuable lessons the talking board can give us, far outweighing the significance of the specific environmental influences we find at work in any particular time and circumstance. Ouija has often advised me to forget *it* and listen to its messages. In the same way, we'll benefit by noticing the message of connection and communication behind the details that form and influence the board's words.

Now we'll leave behind such tangible talking board ingredients as moon madness and dust particles, and take a look at possibilities not usually seen as physical at all. First, our thoughts. We've already considered how our thoughts and beliefs may shape not only the device's words but our realities as well. Maybe we can imagine this to be true in some large vague way, but what does it mean as we sit at the board table? Should we make a mental effort to direct the pointer with our thoughts? Should we attempt to control our thoughts, think "positively" or concentrate on the reply we want? You may have guessed my answer is "No." It *is* possible to control the board's performance directly with our conscious thoughts, but then we will have learned nothing. The little board's value lies in its capacity to mix together a great number of disparate ingredients, most of them strangers to our conscious awareness, and present us, out of that jumble, with a surprisingly coherent brew not quite like any we've tasted before. The value of the idea of thoughts forming reality is in *noticing, not controlling*; as it becomes apparent at the board, simply notice the correspondence between your thoughts and the board's replies. As you begin to experience instances of this idea's truth, you will begin automatically to perceive the power in your thoughts, and you'll begin to regard them with the same importance and sense of responsibility with which you view your actions.

This is a largely automatic process, needing our recognition and attention but not our meddling or control. I've found it helpful to visualize my thoughts, as I sit at the Ouija board, as floating in a river that flows through my head. I watch each thought as it flows by, but I can't stop the river or reach in and grab a thought from it. I give each thought my attention as it passes me, and when it floats downriver out of my sight, I let it go completely, and turn my attention upstream again to wait for the next thought. Whatever is valuable about the thought I've just let go will flow by again—there's no need for me to collect thoughts and hold them tight.

In the first chapter we looked at the possibility of people other than the two persons using the board influencing the pointer's replies. What about the influence of people who not only are not present, but are not physically existent at all? Communication with "ghosts" or "spirits" is the best-known use of the talking board and at the same time the least understood. The next chapter, "Oracular Hazards," is the place for *our* critical spirits to emerge and meet the board's versions of spirits. First, though, we'll courteously consider the reality of nonphysical entities as they present themselves, and listen to what they have to say about influences on the device's words from *their* vantage points.

The published accounts of spirit communication through the Ouija board, and my own experience with definite Ouija personalities, *and* the many stories I've heard, all agree about the difficulties involved in this tenuous venture. The spirits say they are just as thoroughly in the dark as we are, that they gropingly experiment with communicating through Ouija and often make a mess of their attempts. They assure us that crossing death's threshold does not impart "supernatural" powers, nor does it necessarily bring clarity or wisdom—death simply marks the beginning of a different realm of experience, and from that realm this physical world often appears as hazy and insubstantial as death's realm is to our vision.

Certain spirits claim to have more facility than others in making the connection between worlds, just as some of *us* may find it easier, but the linking of appropriate corporeal and noncorporeal partners in this venture is a small beginning, leaving many challenges still to be met. Simply zeroing in on the intended receiver of their messages is a big accomplishment for the spirit communicators. As Stephen the spirit explains it:

> A wireless station often picks up messages not intended for it. In the same way our messages are often picked up by earth stations for whom they are not intended. It sometimes happens in such cases that the receiving station gets parts of one communication jumbled up with parts of another. These cross-currents are unavoidable, and the coloring they cause is quite as annoying to us as to you.

"Coloring" is a common term among those who receive communications from that land beyond. It refers to distortions in the message. Any way in which the message as it is spelled out at the board differs from the message as it was intended by the sender can be called coloring. Some coloring is present in every board communication—since wherever the words originate they filter through our minds, our feelings and vocabularies and compulsions, there will be parts of us in every message—but when our assumption is that some nonphysical personality is attempting to spell the words, we will naturally try to minimize the participation of *our* personalities in the formation of the board's message. One conceptual model for spirit communication is that we relax and keep our conscious thoughts from interfering with the device, and that we somehow allow the spirit personality to temporarily inhabit our subconscious minds. The spirit can then use the contents of our minds as raw materials, combine them in his (her? its?) own way and present a message essentially his own rather than ours. Obviously this process provides infinite opportunities for coloring. Stephen tells of a few of them (remember that "receiving station" is his term for the user of the board):

> Coloring occurs not only as the result of the receiving station's conscious mind overruling the subconscious, but also whenever, in the course of communication, the subconscious mind frees itself from our control. Immediately it gives expression to that which is its own thought and experience. In the case of the Ouija board there is the additional possibility of conscious overruling.

When it comes to communicating specific details, the spirits have an even more difficult time, as Stephen goes on to explain:

> It is very hard to get a name through, that of a person or a place. Dates are very hard, and so are all other concrete items. It is a small matter for me to convey through this station an idea that impinges on no association personal to the station. I can dictate my revelation through Joan, unfamiliar as its terms have been to her, with much greater accuracy than I could state through her my old preference in furniture or flowers. Mention by me of any of the familiar things of living would stir immediately a host of her own subconscious associations.

The planchette, a small board that looks like the pointer of Ouija, with a pencil implanted as one of its three legs, can sometimes be a more accurate tool than Ouija when the object of our efforts is spirit communication. The planchette is operated in the same way as the Ouija board, except that it is placed on a sheet of paper and so writes directly with its pencil-leg in one continuous scrawl. Many instances have been recorded of planchette messages written in an *exact replica* of the *handwriting* of the deceased person claiming to communicate, even when the planchette's operators had never seen the communicator's handwriting. A British man with half a century of involvement in psychic investigation told me of an attempt in which he participated to contact a friend's dead father. The four friends, one of them the son in question, sat in a pitch-dark room with their hands on a planchette. The toy made short marks not at all like handwriting and they all thought, as they sat in the dark, that nothing would come of it. When the planchette stopped and the lights were switched on, the three men who hadn't known their friend's father were mystified by the sight of a complicated drawing of an antique German beer stein. The son went to a cupboard across the room, opened it, and returned with a mug that fit the picture's description in every detail—the father's beer stein, of course. The friends considered their attempt a successful one.

You and your partner may never again sit down at the board feeling sure that you are really alone. You may harbor the suspicion, after considering this welter of possible voices, that there is much more going on in and around you than the surface of your awareness reveals. If this is so, if you find yourself wondering what phase the moon is in as you begin a session, or you see your partner glancing over her shoulder from time to time as if she half-expects to catch a glimpse of the *real* author of the board's words, then I'm glad, because my aim in this chapter has been met. It seems that knowledge serves mainly to deepen mystery rather than to erase it. In our Ouija exploration, as perhaps in anything else, the more complexity we bring to our awareness, the more mysterious and exciting, and yes, confusing, too, does our venture become. It is at this point, when we have already cultivated a certain richness and depth in the way we approach Ouija, that it will be most fruitful for us to examine the hazards and pitfalls that may beset us at the board.

CHAPTER FOUR

Oracular Hazards

Undoubtedly, the very fact of development accentuates one's characteristics, both bad and good. One becomes more sensitive to feeling, suffering, impressions of all kinds; therefore, all the more reason to know yourself . . . *before you commence this "opening of the door." It is not the machinations of evil spirits you need fear, but the operation of your own subconscious shortcomings* . . .

You will have nothing to fear from "evil spirits" if you have nothing to fear from yourself.

—GLADYS OSBORNE LEONARD,
My Life in Two Worlds, 1931

That's a fine statement, Gladys, but who among us really lives as if she had nothing to fear from herself? At our talking boards we are allowing the vast unknown to introduce itself and speak to us; we are letting the unconscious contents of our minds surface and spill their secrets. Each of us has hidden away information and experience that we judged wrong or blasphemous or nasty or inappropriate or crazy or somehow contrary to our beliefs. Such information doesn't disappear—it simply slips below our conscious recollection. Augmenting our individual stashes of taboo perceptions are the taboos of our family, social circle, religious group, and eventually of our culture as a whole, all of them backing up our individually rejected perceptions with their power and authority. It's no wonder that when these long-ignored contents of our minds are finally given a chance to speak, often for the first time through the Ouija board, we may respond with a suddenly overwhelming feeling of terror, sometimes not at all connected with what is actually spelled at the board. The first independent movements of the pointer may spark the same fear—"This instrument is out of *my* control. What terrible secrets will it divulge? What demon moves it through me?" Let's look at what it is we fear so much.

Evil is not a subject about which I have any special knowledge; in fact, I'm often confused about its nature and workings. Still, by a combination of experience and inspired guess I can bring a small light into evil's cavern, and with it we can see our way safely around some of the obstacles that have tripped up many Ouija users before us. In Chapter Six when we look at our oracle's origins, we'll see that it began its career with no taint of evil. The reason for this is that it emerged in a cultural context (in China and then ancient Greece) in which many gods were respected, and in which good and evil were intermingled freely and considered equally necessary parts of reality, expressed in the flow of seasons and in the cycles of decay and renewal, death and birth, that are acted out by all that lives. It was the rise of Christianity, with its insistence on just one god—a god who is only male and only good and has no darkness in Him—that forced the separation of good and evil and the creation of a realm of feminine darkness that could hold everything ungodly. The contents of this dark realm were not even to be looked at—they became what we call the unconscious. Of course I'm exaggerating in order to make a point. Of course the unconscious existed in ancient Greece as thoroughly as it exists today; the difference is in the *access* and *interplay* between the lands of the known and unknown.

Now we can see more clearly why use of Ouija has been strongly condemned by those Christian sects that have not simply ignored the oracle's existence; the little board *does* provide an avenue of access to psychic regions the church has turned over to the devil. Many people involved in what is usually called "the occult" (Edgar Cayce prominent among them) have also denounced the Ouija board as a dangerous toy too easily prey to evil influences. The president of London's College of Psychic Science refused to speak with me, or even to peek out his office door at me, when his secretary told him I was writing a book about the Ouija board. He conveyed, through the secretary, his sincere hope that I abandon such a dangerous activity at once. This perspective is basically identical to the church's view and has its roots, and branches too, in the Christian separation of good and evil. Psychics and trance mediums derive their belief systems from the culture in which they live just as thoroughly as do the rest of us.

I hope it's already apparent that I'm not about to advocate embracing evil. Neither do I mean to imply that use of the talking board and personal Christian faith cannot go hand in hand. What *is* important for us to realize in the midst of this little metaphorical history of good and evil is that at least part of what we think of as evil is culturally defined and changes as our culture does, and that a large part of our response to evil and our attitude toward it are also cultural habits and can be changed. We'll soon see that all these considerations will be a great help to us at the Ouija table.

The psychic region called the unconscious has served as a catchall for every imaginable sort of outcast idea and feeling; many of the creatures we'll find roaming about in its darkness, glimpsed in our minds or showing themselves in the board's words, will seem silly distractions at worst, certainly not evil. One of these creatures who appears frequently at the Ouija board is the prankster. He may suddenly subvert our most serious quest for meaning with a joke or sexual pun; he may lead us into what seems to be a revelation of the secrets of the cosmos only to end by telling us that God is a peanut butter sandwich. The prankster can be a vague tendency showing itself in a session, or a definite personality who announces his presence with a particular name and style. He is one aspect of the devil, that element that delights in sacrilege, that loves to take away meaning and scoff at our sincere spiritual yearnings.

There *is* an element of danger here, in talking board pranks that may entertain or annoy us, and perhaps sometimes shock us, but seem ultimately harmless. I'm approaching this "silly" aspect of evil first because here it's easiest for us to see that the danger, the real possibility for destructive or divisive or meaningless action in the world, lies not in the words of Ouija, but in what we do with them. A Ouija story of an imminent Martian invasion of the earth may sound like a threadbare joke to most of us; to one lonely retired man the board's announcement of this coming event brought temporary meaning to a life gone dull, and conferred on him an important imagined role as liaison between Martians and humans. Gullibility and literalism are the vehicles that carry us into such dangerous regions. Though our areas of gullibility may not be so obvious as the Martian ambassador's, each of us has vulnerable points somewhere, points at which, to bolster our sense of personal importance, we may be tempted to read the device's words at face value *only*.

One example of this process at its most charming and naively sincere is shown in a 1919 pamphlet called "The Secret of the Successful Use of the Ouija Board" (technically true to its title, this little book speaks of the "secret" but does not divulge it). It is the work of Clarisse Eugenie Perrin, assisted at the Ouija board by Nellie Irene Walters. Even their names sound gullible. Clarisse modestly introduces the board's words, which make up most of the book, this way:

My vis-à-vis and myself, as the mediums, or rather part of the mechanism through which this work has been dictated upon the Ouija board, did not anticipate any results of a wide, serious or religious nature when we commenced to toy with one, bought unsuspectingly as a game to help the children of the household to pass away the long dark days of an Alaskan winter. . . .

But Heaven, in its wisdom, took practical advantage of the undisturbed evenness of the "electric lines of space" upon which the spirit folk travel, according to their statements, in that vast and weird domain of our own United States. . . .

Since coming to California this past summer, and reviewing the up-to-date literature upon psychic subjects, I am still thoroughly convinced that these dictations, received in the domestic circle in that northwestern corner of the earth, unfaltering in their diction and strength, are the greatest encouragement, fact, and revelation that this world has ever received through the void.

The great encouragement that follows is an account of the adventures of Tom Thumb, who of course is a tiny elf who lives in a Ouija pointer and carries it about on his shoulders to spell the messages. When the Ouija board is not in use, Tom Thumb leaves it for an idyllic life outdoors—"When it is time for me to waken, morning glories ring out their bells to tell Ouija it is morning . . ." The story of Tom Thumb's rather insipid days among the flowers is obviously not harmful in itself; in fact it contains interesting conjecture, intermingled with descriptions of bluebells, about such questions as the role of magnetism and electricity in moving the pointer. The problem enters with Nellie and Clarisse, who, with their willingness to believe every Ouija word as literal and authoritative truth, have gotten just the nonsense they deserved. They began their Ouija work with a very common and unfortunate assumption—that because Ouija spelled intelligible sentences seemingly outside their own knowledge or control, they could unquestioningly believe every word as inspired truth from some source above and beyond them. This is an easy assumption to fall into, since it is helped along by the wonder and surprise we feel when the pointer moves and spells words without our conscious guidance. "But I'm really not doing it! This message *must* come from someone bigger and wiser than I!" It's a natural response and a potentially dangerous one, for while we may *feel* special and righteous as the chosen recipient of a great new revelation, this abnegation of our critical faculties closes us off from ordinary common sense and can give us the illusion that "the spirits" rather than we ourselves are the ones responsible for our actions in the world. Once we've given up common sense in favor of unquestioning devotion to voices conveyed by Ouija, the prankster of our unconscious minds will delight in every imaginary suit of clothes he can persuade us to parade in. Clarisse and Nellie don fictitious garments ever more outrageous as their little book proceeds, from the mild and silly elf stories at the beginning, to the messianic zeal and biblical language of their final Ouija message: "Verily, verily, I say unto you—sayeth I, a holy spirit, thou hast at last discovered God's true and only telegraph to eternity."

Other users of Ouija have parted with common sense when the departed spirits of famous persons have unexpectedly put in an appearance at the board; several of these doubtful messages have even made it into print. One is a syrupy and half-literate book of trite and repetitious sermons supposedly delivered to the Ouija board by philosopher William James —a glance at James' articulate before-death writing will amply illustrate the hazards of suspending critical judgment of the board's fruits. Another more entertaining blunder is a book by psychic investigator Hester Travers Smith, appropriately called *Oscar Wilde from Purgatory*.

"Spirits" of any description are a potential talking board hazard because they often appear at the board in such convincingly idiosyncratic and individual fashion, sometimes offering verifiable facts we think we couldn't possibly have already known, that it's easy for us to accept their reality at its most concrete level, and from there believe everything they tell us as literally true also. Even if we choose to believe that a once-embodied personality addresses us at the Ouija table, we have no justification for swallowing whatever the spirit tells us without so much as raising an eyebrow here or there. "Stephen," who claimed to be just the sort of spirit we're now considering, had valuable advice to give on this subject:

> If we accept the fact that physical death does not affect the identity of the individual, it will be a necessary inference that there are as many intellectual and moral differences among spirits as among mortal men. . . . Beyond the mere fact, therefore, that spirits live and act (and what greater fact could we ask?), the teachings of spirits are to be received just as we receive those of fallible mortals, and to be subjected to the test of our own spiritual and rational powers. Pressed on by influences from all sides, we are yet to accept or reject them, according to the light which conscience may shed.

I've found that I can often sidestep the oversimplifications of literalism by approaching Ouija messages as if they were dreams. We don't expect the characters and events of a dream to speak to us in a literal, logical way or to have only one meaning. My Uncle Jack can be himself in my dream, carrying on in his usual volatile temper-tantrum style; at the same time he can represent the angry part of me that I seldom express directly; he can in the same dream be a wrathful personification of God berating me for my shortcomings. Just so a "spirit" speaking to us through the Ouija board can have its reality spread across many possibilities at once—a little of one metaphor, more of another, maybe a bit of literal truth too. Ouija messages come to us as dreams do, presenting us with inexplicably familiar mysteries as we watch, relaxed and without judgment, from the windows of sleep or our seat at the Ouija table. It is only later, when we wake up or the message has been spelled out, that we look critically and attempt to unravel some meaning.

The appearance of evil at the Ouija board need alarm us no more than evil in dreams alarms us. If I dream of falling down a flight of stairs, I don't assume the dream is telling me this is about to happen in my waking life. I may be more than usually careful on stairways the next day; if the dream's vividness impressed me sufficiently, I may check the steps leading up to my house for loose boards. Even as I take these precautions, though, I'm aware that the dream's message goes beyond this literal level. I don't remain preoccupied with real stairways, but instead pursue the metaphor of falling, what the image evokes in me, what it reminds me of, what associations it leads to. The ambiguity of dreams helps us see them on many levels at once; the immediacy, the real physical movement of the pointer, the board's use of words rather than pictures, all help us to take its messages literally, to forget that they are layered in metaphor just as dreams are. Thus we are likely to react to the statement of the board that a close friend is dying of cancer in a way very different from our reaction to the same message presented in a dream. We know that in dreams we can die and still wake up in the morning, that we can kill someone and then watch them get up and walk away. Ouija messages come to us from the same darkness our dreams call home.

At the risk of frightening a few people away from the Ouija board entirely, I'll bring out the most extreme illustration I know of the hazards of Ouija literalism. Jane, an intelligent older professional woman whose talents and accomplishments were in her view (and mine) never fully appreciated, began to use the Ouija board at an empty, lonely time in her life. Her closest friend had just died; her career had hit the doldrums; people near her had disappointed her. Ouija told Jane that she deserved a far better situation than the one in which she found herself, and of course Jane agreed. Since the board's words always amplified her own perceptions, offered her solace and acknowledged her worth to a degree no one else did, the game quickly became her most trusted friend. As her enthusiasm grew, Jane found she could operate the board and pointer by herself, and soon she was spending long hours alone with her Ouija "spirits," who called themselves by mythological names comfortingly familiar to Jane from her lifelong study of classical mythology. The gods and goddesses of the Ouija board told Jane that she too was a goddess—and here we've come to the difficult part of this story. Jane's Ouija voices said her unhappiness came from trying to live with mere humans when she really was a goddess. Her troubles would end if she'd only come and live with the gods. Then the voices accused her of playing with their confidence—if Jane truly believed in Ouija spirits, they told her, she should prove it by taking her gun from the drawer and shooting herself. She did.

It seems that we're back to Gladys Leonard's opening to this chapter: "You will have nothing to fear from 'evil spirits' if you have nothing to fear from yourself." And we're back to my response: fears and weaknesses belong to every one of us, whether they show themselves in suicidal tendencies or in simple vanity. This doesn't mean that Ouija "spirits," real or concocted, have any power over us, nor does it mean we should drop our boards and run at the first shady message. Every statement of Ouija we consider "evil" is attempting to bring us a vital lesson. Even Jane's voices from the board urging her to kill herself were not evil in themselves, but were telling her with the strongest possible metaphors that she desperately needed to begin her life again, to end an old way of being in the world and find a new way. Many possible responses were there for Jane to choose from. She could have been jolted from her self-pity by the demand for "proof" of her belief, and with the energy of that jolt she might have taken some constructive action toward easing her isolation. If she had been willing to admit at least partial responsibility for the creation of her voices, she could at least have looked more directly on her desire to end her life. Jane's use of the board illustrates an unlikely extension of the twin hazards of the board: reading messages at their most literal level *only*, and placing responsibility for the board's words outside ourselves.

We can safely avoid misfortunes both disastrous and trivial at our game boards by cultivating an attitude toward talking board activities that is a combination of detachment and responsibility. It sounds (and is) paradoxical, but it is also effective and simple. Detachment at the start of a session allows the creatures and concepts of the dark unknown to move out our fingers into words with little interference from our conscious minds. So many different voices within us and without us may be forming the words, and so many levels of meaning may be possible, that we needn't feel alarmed or disappointed or especially identified with *anything* that is spelled. Sorting out meanings can come later. This act of distancing can also aid in our constant intention to see beyond the most literal, obvious meaning of a Ouija message. At the same time we're detaching ourselves from identification with particular Ouija meanings, we need to keep in mind our participation in the board's creation—this also helps us look beyond literal meanings. A spirit may be sending us a message, but we have sent for the spirit. Whether creating it in the kettle of our unconscious minds or calling out through the ether for a nonphysical personality who resonates to our particular needs, it all comes down in the end to the fact of our responsibility for the device's words.

By keeping enough distance from the board's words to allow for many possible meanings, while at the same time remembering that every message is for and about *us*, sent from unknown parts of ourselves, we'll not only avoid the obstacles we've peered at in evil's cavern, but we'll find every Ouija session much more valuable. We'll not be easily disappointed; we will, with a little practice, be able to see many layers of meaning unfold at once from the words of Ouija. We can be sure that we won't stumble into Ouija hazards, by remembering to watch our reactions and tendencies to literalize especially carefully when certain things happen at the board: when definite personalities, "spirits," claim to speak to us; when Ouija flatters us excessively; when any statement is said to be a revelation or "the only truth" or a message that only we are privileged to receive; and especially important, whenever a voice of Ouija *tells us to do anything.*

What has become of evil in these pages? We seem to have gone round it rather than straight through. We've emerged from the dark cave after having looked at each obstacle we found there and learned how to avoid it in our future Ouija explorations. At each obstacle we've paused, asking: "Is this evil? Is this it? Where does evil live?" And each time we've had to say: "No, evil doesn't reside in the Ouija board. No, the prankster is not really evil. No, even spirits who tell us to commit suicide are only delivering a message we've requested. Evil doesn't find its home in them." We see the appearance of evil—that's all we can say about it. Could it be that's all there is?

I bring out this conjecture because our concepts about evil will affect our experience at the Ouija board. If we were to believe that evil lived in the talking board pointer, a diabolical Tom Thumb who could push the pointer about as he pleased, then our reactions to the oracle's words, and the words themselves, would take on a very particular flavor and content. If we believe that, in some way we might never understand, evil can have no power over us even though we see the appearance of evil all around, then our scope and freedom at the Ouija board will broaden considerably, and we'll use much less of our energy defensively, keeping up barriers at the gates of the unconscious.

Ouija itself has provided metaphors to help us imagine how evil might indeed appear to exist, and yet not exist in an ultimate, indestructible sense. Stephen, the voice of Ouija

we'll hear more from in Chapter Seven, said: "Cold is merely
the absence of heat; darkness the absence of light. Evil is
the nondevelopment of good." You may not go for this; I
myself find that darkness and cold, and evil too, can sometimes feel like very palpable substances. This image can still
help us relax at the Ouija table, though, even if it's laid on
top of a tall belief-pile of images of evil's power and reality.
Another glimmer of light Stephen offers is his emphasis on
Christ's injunction to "resist not evil." This is an idea echoed
by many psychics: our attention to evil, even if that attention be resistance, creates evil or gives it power. We need
to acknowledge the existence of whatever we see as evil,
give it the right to exist in our universe, see that it has a
message for us, and look in the direction we want to travel
rather than back at the obstacles and fears.

My own Ouija experiments have included many sessions
spent in dialogue with the little board over the nature of
evil. What has emerged is a perspective similar to Stephen's,
in which evil as a conscious power does not exist. Voices
I have received through Ouija have equated evil with ignorance, emphasizing that destructive actions are always accompanied by some belief that makes the action *seem* justi-
fied in the eyes of the evildoer, whether the belief be called
"national security" in the case of the Watergate criminals
or "Aryan superiority" in Nazi Germany or "revenge" for
a jealous lover. Our awareness of such justifications is not
meant to do away with evil or make it less than it is. This
concept *does* banish evil from its place as a power outside
us, and makes it instead into the force of ignorance, which
is accessible to us and can be changed by us.

The small lanterns we've acquired in this chapter will be
enough to light our way safely through any dark passage
Ouija may open to us, if we only remember to use them,
so we'll leave evil's cavern behind us now and go on to
explore the myriad possible topics Ouija can bring us. I'll
close our discussion of evil with a metaphor from my Ouija,
which can serve as the vehicle taking us from our emphasis

on evil back to a wider perspective in which evil's small place is apparent in a larger whole.

Ignorance and knowledge are a balancing vine catching the support and falling away in the wind, again and again. But the vine always grows.

CHAPTER FIVE

Everything to Do With Everything

Ouija is not the ground of your beings, nor the seeds of the new life you bring into the world, not the constant sun, but water, *the unpredictable nourisher.*

—Author's Ouija Board, 1977

Almost every user of Ouija I meet has discovered some novel use for the board, whether it be picking racetrack winners or supplying missing historical details for a biography of the Roman emperor Diocletian. You will undoubtedly come upon ways to use Ouija that are not mentioned in this book, and that perhaps have never before been tried. There are so many possibilities that I'll make no attempt to cover them all (I can't even imagine them all). Instead I'll point out general directions our Ouija explorations can take. I'll map the main rivers of this region and each of us can raft up whichever of the countless tributaries attracts us most.

This chapter is a simple geography lesson. We won't concern ourselves here with the river's source or the nature of water; we can wonder at a stream that seems to flow uphill, but we won't search for its secret. We'll learn *how* to float in this dark water, *how* to navigate these most mysterious of rivers, but we won't be asking *why* we float or what it is about the Ouija board that steers us through rapids and shallows. All these questions will suggest themselves as we consider such Ouija topics as finding lost objects or predicting future events. We'll just let the "whys" churn about in our minds for a while, and hope that by the time we arrive at chapters Eight and Nine, where such questions belong, answers will have congealed, as does cream into butter.

We'll start with predicting the future, both because it's an immensely attractive topic and because the last chapter's precautions, still fresh in our awareness, are crucial to our understanding and success here more than anywhere else in our Ouija explorations. A majority of all talking board disappointments and frights involve predictions made by the oracle. The pointer may spell out dismal forecasts about the international political situation, or it may say your best friend will catch the newest flu strain and die from it next winter. Many people are frightened away from using Ouija further by such gloomy news, especially if any of the board's predictions actually happen. On the other hand, many more people give up on the Ouija board when its predictions *don't* come true; they feel their time has been wasted or they've somehow been tricked by unreliable voices of Ouija.

We'll avoid disappointment and fright, and be on the way to finding valuable information about the future and ourselves, by remembering the last chapter's lessons about the hazards of gullibility and literalism. To learn as much as possible from Ouija messages about the future, we also need to understand a bit about how Ouija gets its information. Can anyone's voices received through Ouija somehow really *know* what will happen two weeks from now? If so, our wills are not free; we can't change our futures by the choices we make; the future is determined for us by some force beyond our reach. Determinism is a belief about the way life works. The other side of the argument, free will, is also a belief. The debate between them has gone on for thousands of years and will no doubt continue for thousands more, because the truth of neither position can ever really be *proven*. Maybe free will and determinism do not make a duality at all, but are both true at once, as so many issues that seem to be at odds turn out to be when we understand them more fully (we explored one in the last chapter, the attitude of simultaneous detachment and responsibility). Certainly we all experience both sides of this coin in our day-to-day lives; we sometimes are very aware of destiny's pull on us, and at other times we feel surrounded by choices that are ours alone. To our logical minds, there is an impossible paradox here. Put logic aside, and the paradox suddenly becomes easy to live with, for we all know we have *experienced* both free will and determinism as fully true. Let's take a look, from this newly acquired vantage point, at Ouija predictions of future events.

If our destinies are determined, the plots of our dramas already known *somewhere*, we can assume that with the Ouija board we may possibly be able to gain access, at times, to knowledge of future events of our lives or future worldwide events. This can account for the unlikely details sometimes predicted correctly, the wild improbabilities that could not have been Ouija guesswork. You *know* you'd never buy the yellow sandals Ouija has described as part of your costume on the summer day you'll meet the love of your life in Florence, but when your aunt gives you yellow sandals as a bon voyage gift you begin to look at the oracle's story in a new light.

Unfortunately, the yellow sandals worn on vacation in Italy are quite likely to be the only part of the forecast to materialize as predicted. One reason for this can be seen in the plethora of influences acting on the Ouija users in every session, jumbling the message a bit here, exaggerating there, perhaps letting "yellow sandals" through undistorted because it has no emotional charge, but bringing Ouija users' present hopes and fantasies into play for a romantic fabrication of the future. Possible influences and sources of distortion in the *present* should always be considered when we ask the board about the future.

The other difficulty involved in predictions of the future lies in determinism's mirror image, free will. Ouija personality Stephen puts it bluntly: "It is because your wills are free that fortune-telling is futile." Even though we're assuming, from our limited experience, that there *is* a course laid out for us to follow through this life, we are *also* assuming, based again on experience, that we can change our course at any time by choices we make. In almost any forecast, many particular choices made by many different people are necessary to assure the predicted outcome; one different decision made by just one person in the time that elapses between the prediction and its manifestation can be enough to change the look of the future entirely.

What good is fortune-telling, then, if it isn't really possible? Its greatest value may lie in what it can tell us about the *present*. Assuming that environmental influences on the board's behavior are for the moment minimal, the little board's assessment of the future remains the product of a complex distillation of innumerable factors belonging to past and present, factors too many, too complicated, and too close to us for us to be able to sift them all together *consciously* and arrive at predictions as insightful as the board's. When we sit at the Ouija table and ask about the future, we can imagine this process set into motion: everything both Ouija users know of the past and present situation is considered, and all possibly relevant details are collected and set apart where they can be weighed and played with and rearranged into various combinations. Our feelings about the matter in hand are brought out into view, our hopes and fears and desires. The master plan of our destinies is consulted. Half-formed fantasies we may harbor about this future are paraded out of their hiding places and added to the now substantial collection of contributing factors. The hopes and fears and destinies of other people involved in this particular future are found somewhere, or at the least the *projections* of Ouija players' hopes and fears are located. The unexpected, the paradoxical, the improbable ironic twist of events are all taken into account. From all this and perhaps more, a single future is distilled and its outlines spelled out at the Ouija board. The whole process may take place in a matter of seconds.

What we finally receive is a forecast of the most *probable* future *at the time we consult Ouija.* Five minutes from now the same question may merit a different prediction. In two days we may approach the question itself in a different style. The board's statements about the future reflect back on the present in which they are made. If we remember this we'll be less concerned about whether or not a Ouija forecast comes true, and we'll find more in those forecasts than little tests of the oracle's powers.

It's generally true that the less we "test" Ouija for psychic powers of any variety, the more valuable and interesting our results with it will be. Psychic phenomena just don't seem responsive to the usual scientific methods of investigation, as researchers in what's now called parapsychology are quickly finding out. Darby and Joan, Ouija users who brought "Stephen" into communication with this world, attempted for a while to receive verifiable evidence of Stephen's life before "graduation" (his term for death). They concluded that "the more one sought evidence the more trivial were the messages received." This brings us to another reason for my repeated recommendation that we look for many layers of meaning in each Ouija message: such a sidelong approach to the sometimes fickle psychic realm actually assures more successful results than does a straightforward attempt. When we are prepared to read the board's predictions for the future as metaphors about the present, we increase our odds on receiving accurate predictions. Perhaps we've stumbled into a universal principle of perversity here, the same one that's at work when you try unsuccessfully to coax your toddler into saying in front of company the new word he's been repeating over and over all day. Whatever the reason, it's true that especially when we advance into more obviously psychic areas we'll do better if we turn our gaze a bit to one side and at least pretend, but hopefully really believe, that we're not looking for anything in particular.

All our activities with the Ouija board have a psychic component, in that there is always something beyond the physical and the known and the explainable at work in the pointer's movements. The areas I'm calling most obviously psychic are those topics that not only involve unknown parts of our minds and psyches, but seem to involve forces larger than our individual beings. Fortune-telling is one such area. Another one especially suitable for Ouija board experimentation is telepathy, sending messages from person to person by means of thought alone.

A gentle way to begin telepathic explorations with the board is to ask the board what some absent friend is doing, rather than jumping into the friend's head and asking for her thoughts. Pick people for whom you feel a strong emotional tie, as this will help, and elicit as much detail as you can from Ouija: what is your friend wearing? where is she? what colors and objects surround her? are other people present? in what sort of mood does your traveling Ouija find her? Be sure to note the time and write down all the board's clues. Then compare your oracular version of your friend's activities with her own. Especially if your Ouija account was well furnished with detail, some of it is apt to be correct, and often the least likely bits and pieces. Remember that the "untrue" parts of the message can be just as valuable for you as the true parts, and give your attention to them accordingly.

My unprovable but nevertheless firm opinion is that there is really no danger here of intruding on anyone's privacy. If for any reason I don't want a particular person to know by extrasensory means what I'm doing or thinking, I *auto-matically* create a barrier around myself, like static blocking radio reception, that keeps out that unwanted perception. I don't have to consciously imagine such a barrier; I don't even have to know anyone is trying to read my thoughts. My friend Rob and I were surprised recently when we asked, via Ouija, whether his wife Nan might be ready to consider reconciliation. (She had moved out three months earlier in an energetically furious state of mind, and had refused to speak with Rob since.) The pointer had been strolling casually about the board to answer our previous questions, but as soon as we mentioned Nan the little piece of plastic took off. It jerked and skidded across the board as if it were being thrown with *somebody's* full force. After a few minutes it seemed to have calmed down enough to spell; it made its statement quickly and then shot off the end of the board. The pointer had spelled "Stop meddling with me." We did. It's a good idea, as a matter of etiquette, to include a request for permission from the person whose thoughts or actions we are about to probe just *before* we ask Ouija for information about them. If we're going to assume for the moment that communication of another's thoughts to us through the Ouija board is possible, we may as well also assume that *our* thoughts can reach that other person, at least on an unconscious level. Asking permission will thus assure the person questioned that our intentions are honorable and we don't want to harm them. It also reminds *us* that we can't receive any information *anyway* without the other's permisson. Besides these fine reasons, there's often laughter to be found in the improbable courtesy of "May I read your thoughts?"

Ouija telepathy is a river with many tributaries. You may want to arrange experiments in communication more conscious than simply listening in on someone's thoughts. A friend across town, or across thousands of miles, can sit down to think to you at exactly the time you hold your Ouija session. You may want to attempt a Ouija conversation, with simultaneous Ouija sessions in different places. Some players receive interesting communications from sleeping persons. You can even try interspecies telepathy, though verification will present a challenge. I've gotten surprising and sensible answers to such questions as "What would my dog Kiffy want to say to me if he could speak?" ("Stop laughing at me—it hurts my feelings") or, "Do any of the garden plants have something to say?" ("We broccoli would like you to mulch us.") Perhaps you're beginning to see that the possibilities are endless.

Mention of advice from my garden plants points out the little board's usefulness in practical, everyday affairs. I *did* mulch the broccoli on the strength of the board's suggestion; for matters of greater consequence I would be sure to find additional opinions before acting. In many mundane matters, though, following the board's suggestions can't possibly cause any harm, and *may* be very helpful in saving us time and energy or bringing an important oversight to our attention. I've found the Ouija board especially useful for finding lost objects around the house. Almost every day I misplace something crucial, and though I can't *remember* where I last saw the whatever-it-is, I know that really I *know*; I was the one to set it down and then put a pile of something else on top of it. Ouija can often bring the location of the missing object back up to conscious awareness —unless I really don't want to remember, in which case the board may be able to tell me why I don't want to.

Ouija can also tell us about invisible characteristics of objects we *do* have in hand. This is a standard practice in the psychic repertoire and is called psychometry. A person sensitive to receiving such information from objects can hold in her hand an object with a long history, an heirloom brooch or maybe a Chinese jade elephant, and tell us who owned it when, where it has been, what emotional dramas the person who owned it took part in, etc. The Ouija board can amplify our latent talents in this area. We can hold or touch an appropriately old or experienced object, or set it on the Ouija board if it is small enough, and watch its story unfold.

I was introduced to this possibility one evening when I agreed to sit in on a session of two friends using Ouija. Walt and Irene had been using the board regularly for several months with steadily improving results, until that week, when the pointer had begun to slide off the board into Irene's lap almost every time she touched it. They couldn't get the pointer to stay on the board long enough for it to tell them what was going on, and when Walt and I tried, it simply scooted off the board in Irene's direction. Irene insisted she had no secrets to divulge, and no sudden changes in her life that week. I asked her if she always wore her jewelry for the sessions—three rings and countless silver bangles on her left hand, two more rings and a heavy silver and turquoise Navajo bracelet on the right—yes she did. Still, all that jewelry intrigued me, as it did whenever I saw Irene, so I asked her to take off one piece at a time and set each one down on the Ouija board, as Walt and I sat with the pointer under our fingers. My request really had little or no "psychic flash" to it; I was merely providing entertainment for my eyes, while my attention wandered over my plans for the next day. I was jolted back to the present by a sudden buzz, almost like a mild electric shock, in my fingertips. I looked down as the pointer began to spin circles about the heavy Navajo bracelet, knocking rings and silver circles out of its path and onto the floor. With Irene and Walt back at the board and the bracelet enthroned on the word Ouija, the pointer began a long tale of the bracelet's maker, a Navajo whose name jumbled into a different nonsense syllable at each of the pointer's attempts to spell it. According to Ouija, when this man had died a week before, he had immediately set out to find this particular bracelet. Of all the hundreds of pieces of jewelry he had made, he had kept this one bracelet for almost twenty years—until it was stolen. To the end of his life he wondered what had become of it. Unfortunately, Ouija wasn't able to trace the bracelet's path from the time it left its creator to the day it attached itself to Irene's arm, probably because none of its subsequent owners had a strong emotional link to the bracelet. Irene, enthusiastic and voluble on any occasion and especially so on this night, apparently convinced the bracelet's maker that she would be an appreciative and appropriate heir to it, for Walt and Irene's Ouija sessions have continued smoothly since then and Irene *always* wears the bracelet.

We seem to have turned again into mysterious Ouija waters, after a brief paddle up the stream called "Ouija Board Household Hints." That's how it is in this country—even the most ordinary shallow trickles we can find lead quickly to roaring rivers so dark we can't see their depth. We may as well go on into the mystery. Perhaps the most thoroughly baffling area for Ouija exploration is the matter of communicating with spirits (or nonphysical entities, or now "dead" but once living people). We've already taken a look at problems and considerations peculiar to this topic in the last two chapters. We've seen the difficulties the spirits claim to experience in reaching us, and we've become well acquainted with the dangers of accepting any spirit's reality or messages at their most literal level only. Now we're prepared to remember that spirits may not be *all* metaphor; there just might be a speck of real spook to them after all.

It's especially frustrating to *search* for Ouija spirits. So many variables are involved in bringing their communication across to us—twice as many different factors as in Ouija messages from parts of ourselves, since the spirits are persons as complex and variable as we are—that the most we can do if we want to communicate with nonphysical beings is to keep an attitude of openness and welcome toward them. If we are open to their presence at the Ouija board, nonphysical entities *will* tune in on us sooner or later. Of course, if we *don't* want such communication, that too is automatically clear to any spirits wandering past our boards, and we'll be left in peace. We can detect any attempts at spirit communication by periodically asking Ouija who is speaking to us, and following up any definite or unusual replies with further questioning about the speaker's identity. Fascinating stories often emerge, bringing details of life in a medieval nunnery or tales of nomadic adventure in the Far East of two thousand years past. Occasionally there will be spelled out a more recent life story that can be checked against a town's birth records for its authenticity. Inconsistencies and contradictions within a story are common and simply show that some parts of the communication are coming through with distortion; don't give up because of these slips. And remember that whether you are subconsciously making up the board's story or receiving the words of an autonomous being, the message spelled out is for *you* and reflects your cares and wishes and eccentricities. The involvement of a "spirit" in replies from Ouija does not lessen our participation in and creation of the pointer's words. It simply adds another dimension of meaning to those words.

I've already mentioned the possibility of delving into past and future lives with the Ouija board. If you haven't yet tried it, please do, as this area tends to be one of the most responsive to Ouija exploration. One useful approach is to ask for information on whatever past life is the biggest influence on your present life, or whichever lifetime you can learn most from now. It can also be interesting to search out past life connections with your present family and friends; whether or not your mother really *was* your husband last time around, the statement may lead to important insights about the nature of your relationship with her now. *Again* I'll say, remember the many layers of meaning in every message—and especially when asking about *future* lives, remember that the replies are always *possibilities*, not inevitable truths.

Last chapter we found it helpful to consider the ways the board's words are like dreams—their mystery and mixed metaphors, their habit of speaking to and from many of our parts at once. We guessed that Ouija messages and dreams may have a common source, or at least that their sources overlap at important points. Because of these similarities, our dreams make a fine starting place for Ouija inquiry. The Ouija board can often help us remember the night's adventures by spelling out a dream's main images or themes—this works especially easily when we already remember at least one image (or sound or smell or color or feeling) from the dream. One morning my dreams left only the memory of a hard orange color surrounded by blue. That evening when I asked Ouija to elucidate, it spelled out "orange rock in ocean," and suddenly I recalled the experience of clinging to the orange rock in a turquoise sea while over my right shoulder I watched the approach of a gigantic wave.

Once Ouija has delivered the dream's memory to us, we can go on to explore its meanings. Since Ouija often speaks to us in dream language anyway, with metaphors and stories rather than abstract concepts, its explanations of our dreams are often oblique, piling metaphor upon metaphor, rarely offering the simplicity of traditional approaches to dream analysis. Even if we're familiar with the terminology, we're not likely to receive "The rock is your ego, the ocean the unconscious; you are afraid your ego will be submerged in the power of the unconscious." Our Ouija voices are too close to the dream to tolerate such deadeningly unimaginative interpretations, however true they may be. We're more likely to receive another story, another dream to compare with the first: "Driving a country road, you come up over a hill and see that not far ahead the road ends at a precipice. The cars before you haven't seen this and are sailing over the cliff as they reach it. You can't see past the cliff nor hear the cars crash anywhere below." Or Ouija will ask questions of *us*: "What do you feel as the wave approaches? When it reaches your rock, what do you do?" Or the Ouija pointer may *continue* the dream as it did for me: "You hold fast to the rock as the wave crashes over you, and after a few seconds you realize you can still breathe. You open your eyes and find yourself in a vast underwater tunnel, blue-black water swirling about you and a voice, or the echo of a voice, beckoning you from far ahead." This is not dream interpretation so much as it is open-ended exploration of our psyches, using dreams and Ouija as a double diving board into the unknown. We may learn about the meanings of our dreams in this manner; we're guaranteed to learn about much more as well.

Such an approach to dreams suggests many untried possibilities for using Ouija as a tool in exploring that psychic river most often navigated by therapists and every sort of "mental health" professional. One psychologist of my acquaintance is actually experimenting with the Ouija board in her individual counseling sessions, though she is for now an anomaly among her more traditional colleagues, who continue to scoff at such "childish" methods. Dr. Thacker (not her real name, of course) has constructed her own rather antiseptic-looking board and pointer for her own use, in order to avoid some of the "occult" and "spooky" associations the Ouija board suggests. She tells me she sometimes uses the tool with clients as an alternative to hypnosis; deep-buried memories can surface through skillful work with the images and messages the pointer brings, and the method has the advantage of operating while the client remains in a normal waking state of consciousness.

It's easy to see the board's possibilities as a therapeutic tool, whether used within the therapist/client relationship or as an individual aid to purposeful introspection: it simply gives a voice to whatever is unconscious in us. Giving voice to the unconscious is a small beginning to the potentially complicated process of psychic growth and integration, but it is a beginning sometimes hard to find. Ouija could be a valuable timesaving tool here.

Whatever the psychic depth we seek, Ouija can lead us down. We can start with questions about the unknown areas of our present lives: what is my motivation for this sudden desire to change jobs? Where does my vague anxiety come from? What do I really want? Such motivation-probing questions can bring us useful insights and help us move into more fulfilling lives. If we want to look further, those questions can lead to others more obscure and complicated. When I try to find what it is I really want, Ouija may highlight my need to ask that question by presenting two or three conflicting goals I carry about with me at once. Deeper probing may reveal that one set of goals was formulated by my mother, another by me as a reaction against my mother's goals, and the third by some part of myself still a stranger to my days. From here Ouija could carry me back to events in my childhood that illuminate the beginnings of my adoption of my mother's goals, the beginnings of rebellion, and the origin and nature of that third area of ambition I harbor. Remembrance of significant or traumatic childhood events can be evoked at the Ouija board the same way we evoke the memory of dreams, one small image sparking a chain of many more.

The main difficulty we may encounter working with these emotionally charged, potentially very powerful images and memories is that we may not know what to do with them once we've dredged them up. We may feel over-whelmed, or stuck in unhappy patterns, or in some other way unable to integrate this new information positively into the persons we are now. Often Ouija itself will prevent our overdose on introspection by stopping short its revelations before we feel too exposed. We don't need to depend on the board's discretion, though, to feel safe in these turbulent waters, if we follow a few simple procedures here. First, it's especially important to write down every Ouija response *and* every question just as it's asked. Second, go slowly. If you feel a little shaky after a session because Ouija triggered "forgotten" memories about how you wanted to kill your younger brother when he arrived in this world, don't take the subject any further in a Ouija session until you've settled down about it a bit. My third suggestion is an obvious one: your partner is crucial in such an endeavor. A trusted, empathetic Ouija partner can make a lot of difference both in how deep you'll be willing to dive into the unknown, and in how well you'll be able to use what you bring back. Last, but as important as ever: Don't literalize the board's gifts or make hasty conclusions. Ouija approaches our pasts and our psyches as if they were dreams; the information it tosses up on our shores has many meanings and comes from many different depths. Here is where written records of the board's words become useful. We can look back at replies from many sessions and see the common threads of meaning running through separate stories, remembered events, metaphors that, at the time they were received, seemed to refer to nothing at all.

As we unravel our psychic knots, uncover hidden motivations and make the acquaintance of hitherto unknown parts of ourselves, Ouija can do more than provide raw material for us to chew and digest. At any point along the way, we can ask for advice or direction from Ouija about what to do with the bits and pieces of insight it brings us. Of course these suggestions require critical appraisal of their worth. Even so, allowing for the usual Ouija quirks and jokes, we'll find much of the little board's advice helpful and imaginative. This is hardly surprising considering that in this area we're really giving advice to and from ourselves. The parts of us we're not consciously aware of are themselves aware of our conscious parts—they can therefore see a more comprehensive picture of our situation than our conscious minds alone can glimpse, and are likely, assuming undisturbed Ouija communication, to give good advice.

The same principle applies when we turn our attention from the mind's condition to the body's health. Ouija can give us access to all sorts of information about our physical beings that we usually must guess at from the clues our inarticulate aches and pains provide. The unique advantages of Ouija diagnosis and advice in this realm are numerous: the board can respond to physical warning signals so subtle we may not even be consciously aware of them; advice is completely individual, not determined by a set formula that says symptoms A + B = ailment C that requires treatment D; and furthest of all from usual medical practice, Ouija doesn't look *only* at our physical beings, but includes in its examinations everything within its extraordinary reach. Of course I don't advise simply replacing the family doctor with Ouija. The oracle's best use is as a supplement to traditional medical advice, as a way to catch minor ailments that don't need professional treatment, and as an instrument for going beyond the limits of medical science. Here, as in every Ouija tributary, we need to take our common sense along and use it freely.

I began consulting Ouija with medical problems as a last resort. The winter of 1974 found me suffering the daily pain of rheumatoid arthritis, which affected almost all my joints to the point that walking pained my feet and my hands were too stiff and weak for such routine movements as using a can opener. I'd already been to many doctors, including leading specialists in the treatment of arthritis, and the very best I'd been offered was the possibility of maintaining my present level of pain and disability while adding the side effects of the drugs used for treatment. The Ouija board offered no such dismal forecast, but no promise of cure either, nor any astounding new miracle treatment. What it *did* provide was daily advice and encouragement, with real sympathy and no trace of condescension, and, finally, an attention to all factors making up the disease and my response to it: emotional, nutritional, psychic and mental as well as physical. The board's approaches were myriad. I received detailed advice about diet, with complete menus and instructions for vitamin supplements. Before starting the board's regimen, I looked for confirmation of the soundness of this advice, and found that many of the suggestions of Ouija were echoed by the few nutritionally-aware doctors I could find, and by recent reports of nutritional healing as it is practiced in Europe. A few of the board's suggestions were mirrored only in the newest, still highly experimental data derived from tests with arthritic mice, such as the little board's insistence that I increase my copper intake. Ouija said I needed more of this mineral because "copper conducts electricity from cell to cell."

I was instructed to walk for several hours every day, which I did even though at first each step was painful, as the joints of my feet and ankles were swollen with excess synovial fluid. Some Ouija sessions were spent delving into the psychosomatic aspects of the illness, and ways were suggested for me to deal with it on an emotional level. Some days Ouija told funny allegorical stories. Many times I was simply admonished to love myself, or to concentrate on the ways I was already healthy rather than on the sickness. I found this exercise especially helpful:

> When you awaken each morning, lie in bed and look for your health. Find whatever feels healthy and put your attention there. Feel the light and energy moving through your body. Give your attention totally to the health that is *here now* for five minutes. Remember this feeling at moments of rest throughout the day. Repeat for five minutes before sleep at night.

Though I don't credit Ouija with the complete recovery that followed—I don't mean to even faintly suggest that the board itself has any curative powers—my experience illustrates one case in which the little board proved a more effective medical adviser than any properly credentialed M.D. Before you venture into this area with your Ouija board, be sure to take a good look at your beliefs about health and medicine. If Ouija diagnosis sounds crazy or dangerous to you, then you very likely *would* create trouble for yourself by attempting to use it.

If you want to ease into a Ouija exploration of the body's wisdom *gradually*, I suggest nutrition as a starting place. Ouija can be an ideal nutritionist, since we each have unique nutritional needs, and who could know those needs more intimately than our own unconscious selves? I make a habit of asking Ouija periodically about my nutritional needs, because I find that, at least according to my oracle, those needs can change quickly and drastically. Laurel used the board's advice to lose extra pounds; though she had tried many diets and heard of many more, Ouija brought suggestions Laurel hadn't heard of, suggestions that *worked* because they were individually created for and from the one who knows best what Laurel needs.

The fields of medicine, nutrition and psychology could all become fascinating streams for Ouija experimentation by open-minded people with special expertise in those fields. All of a doctor's specialized knowledge and vocabulary would be available to the pointer, making possible an exactness in the body's communication that those of us without such knowledge would be less likely to reach. This is true of any field requiring specialized knowledge. A physicist at the Ouija board might receive information about how the pointer moves, spelled out in terminology more precise and illuminating than our everyday vocabulary can manage. *Whatever* your work or field of interest, it brings an added richness to your Ouija sessions, and Ouija will return this richness by sparking new ideas and reflecting imaginative perspectives back on your field of interest. You may even, as I once did when I sat at the Ouija table in a particularly domestic mood, find yourself copying down unusual new recipes to try, straight from the board's kitchen. Here's one, for an excessively healthful candy that provides all the B vitamins in doses larger than you'll find anywhere. I've come to call it Goo Ball:

> Mix together equal parts peanut butter, honey, and nutritional yeast. Add raisins or nuts if desired. Make into balls and roll balls in coconut.

In every one of these Ouija rivers, we are exploring our own creativity, in and around and through whatever else we're doing with the alphabet and pointer. We're discovering the widths and depths and whirlpools of energy that express themselves through us with the inevitability and natural grace of a bubbly overflowing spring. The idea of being creative is often spoken of as if it were a subject in itself, something one is or is not; our Ouija explorations can give us the *experience* of creating in many different areas and styles, and can show us that creating is what we *all* do, already, in the daily living of our lives. Ouija has had much to say to me about creativity—I'll let it emphasize my point here:

> Creation is not a solemn affair, as you like to pretend in order to make yourselves feel more important. Rather it is what you do moment by moment when you are not interfering with yourselves. Your task is to make conscious your creative process without losing it. Then you will truly be creating your own lives and, collectively, the life of the universe, in ways which are infinitely variable yet always within the web of cooperation that links all manifestations of life.

For me, this awareness—that what we call creativity is simply the process of becoming conscious of what we already are doing—has been one of Ouija's most valuable lessons. So many of us believe we're "just not creative." When we find ourselves spelling out imaginative stories, insightful advice, even clever pranks at the Ouija board, we begin to realize we *are* creative after all. The secret lies in the ability to bring the turmoil of words and ideas up to conscious awareness, and with Ouija we have been developing exactly that ability. Laurel tells me that what she values most from all she has gathered in her Ouija explorations is *confidence*. Once she saw how tremendously creative she was with the little board, and realized Ouija merely gave her access to what was already *there*, somewhere, Laurel felt confident enough to go on writing creatively on her own.

There are many ways we can use Ouija to specifically encourage our creative action in all areas of our lives. We've considered the usefulness of Ouija in giving us advice on personal problems or relationships. This advice is so useful, and often so unusual too, precisely because it is creative; it rises spontaneously from unknown parts of us, flipping our perception so that the problems we brought to the board become vehicles for the creative expression of our unique and powerful dramas. Problems *are* problems, after all, because we're stuck in them. The old ways of getting through the situation aren't working; what's needed is a new perspective, one that has not existed for us before and that we must create. Any area of our lives where we're feeling unsatisfied and believe we don't know what to do can be fertile ground for Ouija watering. A married couple I know, finding their relationship drifting in the doldrums, went so far as to ask Ouija for suggestions about improving their sex life. They received very explicit directions, which incorporated fantasies and needs they both were only dimly aware of and would have been too embarrassed to suggest on their own. They created, at the Ouija board, a painless and fun way through what could have become a major obstacle to their growth together.

Now that we see how creativity is not one subject but the living essence of all we do, we can look at ways Ouija can aid in those areas traditionally labeled "creative" or "artistic." Since the board's medium is words, it is perhaps most directly helpful with writing, though I've also used it successfully as an aid to visual art projects and other sorts of creative work. First, we can come to Ouija knowing we want to work on some project but not knowing where to begin; the oracle can give us ideas, images, even little practice exercises geared exactly to our needs. When I wanted to start painting after a break of several years, Ouija gave me small, not-too-threatening "assignments" for a few weeks to help me regain confidence and keep with it in that awkward period before the process acquires its own momentum. Laurel received similar directions for writing when she needed them, unusual short exercises meant to get her going and broaden the range of what she believed she could do with writing. One day Ouija told her to write a story in the form of a grocery list. The next day she was told to take an actual grocery list and use its contents metaphorically as the basis of a short explanation of the workings of the universe. For a more ambitious assignment, we followed the pointer's directions and tape-recorded one of our conversations; then Ouija directed Laurel to take that conversation and use it word for word in a story, while creating a completely different context around the words. We can look at Ouija as a personal teacher in these waters, and we'll gain even more confidence and ease with the creative work we begin by knowing that this teacher is actually a part of us.

Once we're at work on our own we can return to Ouija when we run aground on a sandbar in the river or lose our bearings in a wide lake. The larger perspective Ouija often brings in such cases, and the reassurance that we are indeed moving with some purpose, can be invaluable. I consulted Ouija in a floundering spirit several times during the early stages of this book; you can judge for yourself how helpful it may have been. Often a general reassurance from the board and a reminder to relax a bit are enough to send us back to our writing desks or easels knowing we can go on. Sometimes, though, Ouija has offered me very specific suggestions about what to do next, what topic to focus on, even what title I might want to use (though, alas, I've coaxed nothing so specific from Ouija concerning this book).

We can even write stories, poems, songs and plays *at the Ouija board*, without consciously composing a single word. Pearl Curran, a Missouri housewife, received dozens of volumes of fiction and poetry this way from Patience Worth, a personality of Ouija. (We'll hear more about her in Chapter Seven.) I've received essays and parables, and occasionally the words to a song that all present were then requested, by the Ouija board, to sing. My current Ouija project is a suspenseful mystery novel, copied down word by word as the pointer spells out a complex, quickly moving drama with many characters and rich detail. I never have any idea what will happen next—I don't even know what the next word will be. This sort of Ouija creation is often accompanied by an eery feeling that whatever work is being spelled out at the board *already* exists somewhere out there in the void in finished form; our job with the board and pointer is merely a matter of taking dictation. I'm fascinated by this feeling and have a hunch that it's an important clue, telling us we're receiving a message with very little distortion (though *not* telling us anything about where the message comes from).

The first time my Ouija board spelled out an entire essay was an overwhelming experience for me. Laurel and I had asked "What is the connection between sexuality and spirituality?" We certainly didn't expect any particular sort of answer, but when the pointer immediately spelled out a title, an introduction, and seven section headings, we were amazed. Where did all this come from? How could it possibly exist *before* it was spelled out at the Ouija board, as seemed to be the case? The entire essay took six weeks of Ouija sessions to complete; it contains 2,000 words, all individually spelled out at the board. The title given by Ouija for the whole production is "The Universe in You: Suggestions for Sexual Syncopation." Here is one section that consists of an exercise I find very useful:

The Smile of a Natural Animal

Find yourself alone in a comfortable and private place with a mirror. Smile. Smile on, and think as you watch yourself smile of all the smiles you smile each day. How does that feel? Most likely terrible. This is not the expression of good will or pleasure, but of fear of one sort or another. Realize now that your beliefs about pleasure are most certainly distorted, are in fact distorted to the degree to which you felt terrible in the above exercise. Think on this for a moment. The margin of doubt you have just acquired will be very helpful to you in experiencing pleasure at the innocent and intense level of the natural animal.

Now, consider the amorphous environment around you, not the objects and feelings connected to them, but such important commonplaces as heat, constriction of clothing on your body, or the feel of the surface you sit or lie on. Imagine you are suspended in sea brine or a gravity-free chamber. Lie down. Take off your clothes or loosen them. Relax and imagine a waterfall flooding through you, taking with it all your tensions and unnecessary or insincere smiles. Watch the waterfall until you are empty of all thoughts and feelings, with only the awareness of your glistening body in the focus of that powerful water's movement. Think on whatever aspect of your creatureliness you feel best about, not what any others value, such as the smoothness of skin or shapely elbows, but whatever brings you the fullest sense of bodily joy and health. Feel this joy and well-being spread to every cell of your body, to those parts that are ill or unloved by you in your usual day-to-day reality. Feel the one integral whole which is you in the body. Know that the spread of health and joy through every cell is not metaphor but solemn physical truth. Concentrate on the joyful song of your body until you can feel the singing in every part of you, until you are pulsating harmoniously. Then, without interrupting your awareness of the music, look again in your mirror. There—the smile of a natural animal.

Just as the exploration of *any* Ouija river teaches us about our creativity, any use of Ouija will also broaden and deepen our awareness of our psychic powers. Few of us believe we're sensitive to receiving information in extra-sensory ways, just as few of us believe we're creative. The board's first influence here is to show us what we already know, and so give us more confidence in our psychic abilities and enable us to see such abilities as ordinary and no longer spooky. Most of the areas we've considered in this chapter involve some mode of receiving information that goes beyond what we think of as the usual range of our senses. As we come to accept these ways of knowing as natural, which happens automatically as we proceed in our Ouija exploration, our psychic abilities will begin to stretch and unfold into the space we've provided for them. Ouija can become a valuable tool for us to use in expanding our psychic abilities, as it takes each of us at our own speed into exactly those areas in which we have most latent ability. This is a natural self-regulating process that happens as we use the Ouija board; we don't need to concentrate on it, nor even to be aware of it except to notice the changes in us from time to time. We'll look at psychic development in detail in the very last chapter, considering then the ways the Ouija board can take us beyond its capabilities altogether, into the realms of trance mediumship or other ways of directly receiving extrasensory information.

Your facility in navigating Ouija waterways that I've pointed out in this geography lesson will improve with experience. Nevertheless, a few of my suggestions are likely to remain dry streambeds no matter how many times you look for them. Others will open up talents you never knew were there; you may discover Ouija swamps and whirlpools I haven't even imagined. Remember that whatever is spelled has *some* meaning, even if it's not the meaning you thought you were looking for. You may have landed in the middle of an unknown Ouija river; stay with it and see where it takes you.

CHAPTER SIX

The Oracle's Origins

The spirit of the law is unchanged and unchangeable, but the letter progresses with civilization's advance.

—MARGARET CAMERON, 1918

Though Mr. Fuld may have thought his design of the Ouija board an original one, it had actually been in use *at least 2,500 years* before he capitalized on it. In a form almost identical to the modern Ouija, the talking board was an integral part of Pythagoras' famed school of philosophy in the Greece of 540 B.C.:

> The brotherhood held frequent séances or circles at which a mystic table, moving on wheels, moved toward signs inscribed on the surface of a stone slab on which the moving table worked.

The participants gathered in a circle about the stone slab; whether or not they touched the moving table with their fingers as modern-day users of Ouija do is not clear from the accounts left us. In any case, the process was taken very seriously by those privileged to participate, and the answers given were interpreted for their prophetic value and for the knowledge of the cosmos they might reveal.

Pythagoras himself did not invent the intriguing apparatus, but brought the idea back from his travels in the East. We can only guess at the board's earlier history. Its use may go back several thousand more years, and its true beginnings will no doubt remain a mystery.

Since Pythagoras' day, the talking board and countless variations on it have been discovered and forgotten many times over. Though the device itself has changed very little, its *accessibility* has broadened so remarkably that Pythagoras would scarcely recognize today's Ouija board.

Pythagoras' "circle" was a very select one, as were other groups of philosophers, rulers, or priests who used methods similar to Ouija. Many times the secret belonged to a single priest/ruler, and often the apparatus itself was considered magical, somehow containing within it the source of the knowledge it imparted. You or I, living in such times, would most likely not even know of the existence of these oracles. If we *had* heard of them, we might be inclined to consider their proprietors very powerful and holy—it would certainly never occur to us that we could ourselves construct a stone slab and a table on wheels and have the same power and knowledge available to *us*.

The rise of Christianity in Europe meant an official end to this sort of magic; if the board's use survived at all it remained a well-kept secret. And later, when the Church's hold began to loosen to secular powers and Science and Reason gained influence, they proved just as efficient deterrents. To the Church, the talking board represented the devil; to the scientists it was superstition and silliness. In either case, the ruling classes were dissuaded from the practice of such barbarian rituals—which opened the way, of course, for barbarians, and everyone else whose conduct was not considered very important. So the board's next appearance was on a scale much broader than ever before and touching many more people's lives.

We'll focus on Europe here, and eventually the United States, because it was out of the Western cultural milieu, western Europe and the U.S. in particular, that the talking board as we know it today emerged. Instruments similar to Ouija were and are used in many other parts of the world, and as we have seen, the oracle probably originated in the East—most likely in China, from what bits of information we can piece together—but our own garden will give us the most for our digging.

Today's Ouija is an improvement upon a device called a planchette, and it is to the planchette's tale we have now come. The planchette is a heart-shaped board about ten inches in length. It balances as a tripod; two of its legs are wheels and the other, at the pointed end, is a pencil. The planchette is placed on a sheet of paper, and when one or more persons rest their fingers on it, the board moves about spelling words or drawing pictures in one continuous scrawl.

We know that the planchette appeared first in France during the 1850's—beyond this, the accounts are wildly conflicting, and seem to suggest spontaneous generation in many different quarters. One investigator reports emphatically that "in 1853, a well-known French spiritualist, M. Planchette, invented this instrument to which he gave his name." This seems quite a coincidence considering the fact that *planchette* is a common French word meaning "little board."

Other accounts of the period stick to 1853 as the year of discovery, but move the scene to Germany. One reporter insists that a German milkmaid came upon the phenomenon when she happened to hold a pencil gripped in a pair of scissors at arm's length, and found that the pencil began to write on a conveniently nearby piece of paper.

More reasonable conjecture points once again to the East. A French explorer returning from China in 1843 reported one practice so common that every household indulged in it. A table or smooth floor was sprinkled evenly with bran or flour. Two people then sat at opposite sides of the powdered area, holding a small basket between them. A reed or chopstick was fastened to the basket so that its point rested in the flour. Then the spirits were invoked by the observers present, and the basket moved about, the trailing chopstick spelling out messages or making signs and pictures the group could interpret.

Even if knowledge of this Chinese custom were not widespread, the planchette could have evolved quite naturally from the phenomenon of table-rapping. Some psychic investigators of the time hold to *this* theory of the planchette's origin. By the 1850's table-rapping was a common procedure among Spiritualists, that growing minority of eccentrics convinced that the dead live on and may communicate with the living. Table-rapping, too, has a long and obscure history, going back at least to the thirteenth century Mongols. For our purposes it is enough to note that it was a well-established method by the time we look in on it, though not so established that it could not be improved upon. The proper etiquette was this: a group of people sat in a circle about a table, their hands palm down on the tabletop and their little fingers touching those of the persons on either side so an unbroken circuit was made. The spirits were invoked and presently the table, or one end of it, rose into the air to signal a spirit's presence. The table legs hitting the floor made a "rapping" noise, which became the basis for all communication from the "spirits" to those present. One rap meant "no," two raps "yes." In this way not only could simple questions be answered, but names and long messages were communicated as well. One of the group recited the alphabet; when the desired letter was reached, the table rapped an affirmative reply. Reciting the alphabet for each letter of each word of each message must have been quite tedious, and no doubt many groups tried different ways to streamline the process.

One logical step, once a group had a responsive table under their hands, was to attach a pencil to a foot of the table and put a piece of paper on the floor beneath it. The next logical step was to use a very small table to begin with, or even a box with a pencil attached to it. It seems that, at first, people wanted the spectacle of a heavy oak table rising into the air to convince them that something beyond the play of their imaginations was indeed happening. After that had been established, they could consider the practical aspects of the communication. Eventually even the box was discarded in favor of a small flat board on wheels—the planchette as it remains to this day.

Oddly enough, it was not in the drawing rooms of admitted Spiritualists that the planchette first surfaced, after its evolution or invention or importation, but in the nunneries and monasteries of France. The little board's use was so widespread among the monks and nuns that in 1856 the Bishop of Paris felt it necessary to issue a pastoral letter expressly forbidding the planchette's use among the clergy. His decree moved the monks and sisters into secrecy rather than abandonment of the "tablet," as many of them called it, and it also had the effect of arousing public interest in the strange phenomenon. Fortunate enquirers began to be admitted as visitors to the now-secret sessions, and soon planchettes were popping up in all sorts of places about Paris, and England as well. Even a few Americans visiting Paris at the time managed to sit in on ecclesiastical planchette parties; at least one, Dr. H. F. Gardner of Boston, returned home with a planchette and began making them for his friends.

All this activity remained, for a while, something of a sideshow in the general hoopla over Spiritualism and psychic phenomena in Britain, France and the U.S. Dramatic and spectacular mysteries had taken hold of the public imagination: European psychics like David Dunglass Home were materializing people who claimed to have lived thousands of years ago, out of the invisible vapor the Spiritualists called "ectoplasm"; in the United States, haunted houses and the Fox sisters were conversational topics familiar to everyone. But it took American capitalism to bring the possibility of personal psychic experience into every home, and make the planchette an instant popular mania.

In 1868 a U.S. toy company decided the planchette's time had come, and in that year the booksellers' shops, small-town general stores and specialty shops were flooded with the toys. Thousands of planchettes sold immediately. Periodicals as diverse as *Lippincott's Magazine* and *The Boston Journal of Chemistry* featured articles on the planchette. Small-town newspapers carried such stories as the *New Albany Ledger*'s "The Modern Prophet: The Capacity of Planchette as a Matrimonial Agent." The *Boston Watchman and Reflector*, a religious newspaper, described the planchette craze this way:

> Planchettes trundle in the windows of the tract-house and tobacco stores, dance among opera scores and Sunday-school books—heart-shaped planchettes, square planchettes, planchettes for eight dollars, planchettes for fifty cents, planchettes of walnut, ash, mahogany, gutta-percha, tin, glass—planchettes on pegs, coils, and pentagraph wheels. Planchette confronts you at the dancing parties and in the minister's study, in the drawing room and the "settin'-room,"—is a substitute for the weather and Charles Dickens in the "social circle,"—and the end thereof, who can foretell?

All this in just one year, 1868. In the same year, two books devoted to the planchette saw publication: *Planchette's Diary*, a young lady's personal account of her planchette adventures, and *Revelations of the Great Modern Mystery Planchette, and Theories Respecting It*, a compilation of many of the magazine and newspaper articles published that year. The next year Epes Sargent's *Planchette; or, The Despair of Science* was translated from its original French and published in America. M. Sargent approached the question of why this sudden interest in Spiritualism and psychic phenomena had hit the Western public in the 1860's:

> The complaint is often made that science has outrun religious belief; that as men have acquired more knowledge, they have become more and more unsettled in their opinions as to their inner life, and in the existence even

of the spiritual world. The facts of modern Spiritualism present themselves no sooner than they are needed to meet the want which this tendency has created.

The scientists themselves, on the other hand, put up an often hysterical, and in every case, irrational opposition to the planchette and the other psychic phenomena of the day. Certainly a good deal more questioning than some of the more gullible true believers allowed themselves would have been helpful, especially questioning about the sources and meanings of the physical manifestations. But the scientific community, on the whole, never got as far as even admitting that any measurable physical event occurred except by tricks on the parts of all those participating; the planchette was *pushed about* deliberately. Several scientific journals publicly lamented this state of affairs and appealed to the scientists' more objective sides. Dr. James R. Nichols wrote about the planchette in *The Boston Journal of Chemistry*:

> There is in scientific circles a peculiar sensitiveness upon the subject; and odium and disgrace are liable to rest on anyone, no matter how high his position may be, who cherishes a belief even in the reality of the physical disturbances.

Other scientific journals published appeals for unbiased investigation of the planchette and chastised those who had been especially prejudiced in their approach to the subject. *Scientific American* cited Professor Faraday, who was offered the opportunity to investigate the celebrated British medium D. D. Home:

> Mr. Home was invited [by Faraday], as a condition precedent to Faraday's entering on the investigation, to acknowledge that the phenomena, however produced, were ridiculous and contemptible.

American scientists conducted themselves with no more dignity than their British counterparts when psychic phenomena were considered. Harvard University organized a rigidly controlled test of two psychics in 1868; after a performance successful far beyond the mediums' expectations, considering the hostile conditions, one of the observers, a Professor Agassiz, had this remark: "I made up my mind before coming here, that nothing would come of it; and I am only the more convinced that it is all deception."

It has taken a hundred years for scientists to come to a more humble outlook and begin the serious study of phenomena beyond the usual range of our senses, but that study has at last begun. (In Chapter Eight we'll look at the results so far reported that may help us understand how Ouija works.) Scientists can now agree with Epes Sargent's rather quaintly expressed view:

> It is the duty of Science to wait upon Nature, to reverently listen to what she chooses to tell, and in the way it pleases her to utter it, and deal with the facts that are manifested without ignoring them because others are not manifested. We must be glad to learn her lessons on the conditions she chooses to prescribe, thankful to accept such insight into her arcana as she vouchsafes to grant.

For those delving into Nature's arcana via the planchette, one drawback to the method soon became apparent: because the pencil was itself one of the planchette's three legs, it couldn't lift off the paper between words. The resultant continuous line of letters, often crossed out when the planchette moved from the end of one line to the beginning of the next, could often be deciphered, but just as often not. So the dial-planchette came into popular use as an improvement.

The dial-planchette was very like a roulette wheel: a circular board with pointer attached at the center. Around the outside of the circle were printed the alphabet, numbers,

YES, NO, GOODBYE and DON'T KNOW. The participants placed their fingers on the pointer, which then traveled the circumference of the circle easily on ball bearings or rollers, stopping on the chosen letters of its message. With someone present to write down the words spelled, this device was as fast as the planchette and completely legible. But it too had its faults.

Some of the dial-planchette's letters were upside down no matter what one's position by the board—a small inconvenience. More irritating was the confusion of the pointer spinning about while two sets of fingers tried to follow it; every full turn, the participants had to either rotate *themselves* about the board or cross their hands over. The positioning of the pointer in the middle and the letters around the outside also meant that the operators' hands were often obscuring the pointer's responses. Obviously the dial-planchette needed to be simplified into the device we know as the Ouija board.

The exact origin of the talking board in nineteenth century Europe is another mystery. The trademark OUIJA, a combination of "yes" in French and in German, suggests an association with those two countries, but no one really knows. The apparatus itself is so simple and ancient an idea that it seems likely it would have evolved naturally from the planchette and dial-planchette, perhaps first appearing in several different places at about the same time. Once again, though, it took the acquisitive American spirit to popularize the idea on a wide scale.

In 1899 William Fuld, an ambitious small-time businessman, designed "OUIJA, the MYSTIFYING ORACLE." Mr. Fuld and his brother, Isaac, marketed the game for years, and ended up by selling their rights to Parker Brothers in 1966.

By the turn of the century the planchette craze was a silly bit of history for most people who remembered the notoriety it received in 1868. The media had dropped the subject after their initial interest—science had been unwilling to enter the debate, and few publications were willing to seriously discuss the *content* of planchette messages—in fact, not a single U.S. newspaper or magazine carried a story on the planchette after 1869. Dedicated spiritualists still experimented with the planchette, and many more people knew what it was, but the "popular mania" had definitely evaporated. It's no surprise that when the Ouija board was first put on the market in 1902 it attracted little attention. It was not until the First World War ushered in a sudden and urgent interest in life after death that the Ouija board caught on in a big way.

All the methods anyone had ever heard about for communicating with "the other side" proliferated during the war. Professional and volunteer mediums were in constant demand for the solace they could attempt to bring to grieving widows, mothers, and sometimes fathers—a few characteristic remarks, perhaps even something "evidential," to convince them their sons or husbands still lived, though in another world. Many who could not or would not go to a medium *did* try to contact their loved ones by means of the Ouija board, and some received answers convincing enough *to them* that they were able to put their grief in perspective and go on with their lives.

As Ouija became more widely known, many people with no motive but curiosity began to experiment with it. This was especially prevalent in the U.S.—in France or Britain it might have been hard to find anyone not personally touched by the war's losses. Predictably, the "merely curious" had results with Ouija that were very different from the "personal messages" of the grief-stricken. Shortly after the war it became apparent that these less emotionally involved experimenters had been many and their results various and surprising; a rash of Ouija books was published in the first few years following the war. Stewart Edward White summed up the phenomenon this way:

> The procedure was almost standard. Two people—or a group—fooling with the thing as a lark or out of curiosity. It moves. It becomes coherent. It spells out "messages."

That was the start, the "take-off." What happened after that depended on the people involved. The subsequent proceedings ranged from the "communications" of pure spiritualism to speculative philosophy. Nine in ten of them were spoiled for any serious consideration by what might be called the awed approach that inhibited any common-sense editorial appraisal. This was a pity. After a time even those especially interested in such things became inclined to shy off from "another Ouija board book."

In Chapter Four we looked at some of the more ridiculous products of the "awed approach"; in the next chapter we'll explore the finest "speculative philosophy" to emerge in this phase of the history of Ouija.

By the 1920's Ouija had nearly completed its metamorphosis in the public eye from occult object to curious toy, aided by the demystifying effect of the many new books on psychic phenomena. Organized religions of this country all more or less vehemently opposed the toy. Some ignored it; some, like the Latter-Day Saints, took official positions against it; a few Fundamentalist sects circulated tracts denouncing this "tool of Satan." Sales of the Ouija board climbed steadily; the toy took its place next to the Monopoly® and Scrabble® games on shelves in American homes.

Interest in Ouija, and in psychic phenomena in general, grew at a slow and steady pace from the 1920's up until the sudden spectacular boom of the last ten years. Though Ouija hasn't played a very noticeable part in this newest phase of psychic expansion, it has served as a beginning for the explorations of a number of well-known and now well-developed psychics—Jane Roberts of "Seth" fame among them. There must be a wealth of undocumented exploration going on as well—Parker Brothers has sold more than seven million Ouija boards in the last decade. Can they all be gathering dust beside the Monopoly® set?

CHAPTER SEVEN
Words of Ouija®

*I shall play with words like castanets. I shall
set them twinkling like stars, yea, and make
them pale and languorous. I shall burn them
of passion and wreak them dizzy of twisting.
He who keepeth apace shall find him a lout
at the prancin'.*

—"PATIENCE WORTH," 1915

In this chapter we'll follow the prancing of Ouija pointers
under different hands in different times and places, repeating word for word what Ouija has spelled. If Ouija words
could make a patchwork quilt, then we have just arrived
at the quilting bee. We learned last Autumn how to em-
broider quilting pieces, and we've brought along the ones
we've made so far. We'll begin here to look at the patches
our neighbors have contributed. Who knows what sort of
crazy-quilt will result?

First we'll look to "Patience Worth," a seventeenth century spinster who made herself known through Ouija and
would probably appreciate the idea of a Ouija patchwork
quilt. As you may have gathered from the remarks of hers
I've already quoted, Patience Worth was (is?) a very definite personality, even though she may have had no existence

apart from the Ouija board. Patience first appeared on a summery St. Louis evening of 1913, at the Ouija board of two friends, Emily Hutchings and Pearl Curran. Emily was full of enthusiasm for Ouija, and for over a year had managed now and then to secure Pearl's participation at the board, even though Pearl had no real interest in the toy and the pair's results had been consistently banal. On this evening Emily's persistence finally rewarded her. The pointer revved up its motions and spelled: "Many moons ago I lived. Again I come—Patience Worth my name." After suitable exclamations over this greeting, the two women put their fingers on the pointer again, and immediately the message resumed:

> Wait, I would speak with thee. If thou shalt live, then so shall I. I make my bread at thy hearth. Good friends, let us be merrie. The time for work is past. Let the tabby drowse and blink her wisdom to the firelog.

With that introduction, Patience Worth and her fleshly collaborators began what was to become probably the most prolific and certainly the most publicized series of Ouija board messages ever. In just the first five years of her twenty-five-year-long Ouija existence, Patience Worth spelled out enough words to fill thirty volumes the size of this book. Four volumes of her Ouija words *were* published: *The Sorry Tale: a Story of the Time of Christ, Hope Trueblood*, and *The Pot Upon the Wheel*, all three of them novels, and *Light from Beyond*, a selection of poetry. Much was written *about* the Patience Worth phenomenon as well, with psychologists, linguists, psychic researchers and all manner of curious people attending Ouija sittings, adding up to thousands of onlookers over the years. At the height of the popular enthusiasm there was even a monthly publication called *Patience Worth's Magazine* (it lasted only ten months).

The ladies in charge of all this uproar at the Ouija board

soon discovered that Pearl Curran was the true medium necessary for Patience Worth's emergence; Pearl could sit at the Ouija table with any partner and still receive messages, but Emily had no results at all without Pearl. Patience described the situation thus: "I hae said it be a trick o' throbbin'. The wench be atuned unto the throb o' me." It was clearly *not* a trick of any more obvious sort. Pearl Curran was a thirty-one-year-old middle-class housewife with an eighth grade education and no previous interest in spiritualism or the occult. She was an intelligent woman but unremarkable aside from her connection with Patience Worth. Various investigators of the puzzle quizzed Pearl on her knowledge of or exposure to literature, poetry, history—all subjects well known to Patience—and Pearl's replies showed her to be either too ignorant or too full of grace even to be embarrassed by her lack of knowledge. Pearl regarded her Ouija adventure as a spiritual education, and made the sittings and their results available to as many people as possible without ever attempting to exploit the phenomenon for financial gain. As she described her experience:

> Whatever may be the association which I describe as the presence of Patience Worth, it is one of the most beautiful that it can be the privilege of a human being to experience. Through this contact I have been educated to a deeper spiritual understanding and appreciation than I might have acquired in any study I can conceive of. Six years ago I could not have understood the literature of Patience Worth had it been shown to me. And I doubt if it would have attracted me sufficiently to give me the desire to study it.

Patience Worth's productions did, on the whole, require a bit of study before making complete sense to our modern ears. Her first messages came through in fairly straightforward and simple English, but as her speech became more

familiar to her audience, Patience sprinkled her messages
more and more thickly with archaic English dialect of the
seventeenth century. The poetry, especially, uses words and
expressions and quaint spellings long gone from the English
language. One novel, *Hope Trueblood*, is written entirely
in modern English. Another, *Telka*, uses a combination of
dialects from different parts of England, with not a word
that has come into the language later than the sixteenth
century.

Telka provides a good example of the astonishing literary
stunts that were a large part of the fascination Patience
Worth held for many people. It is a seventy-thousand-word
novel in verse form, and took thirty-five hours of Ouija
board time to produce. Its characters are fully developed,
its plot well planned, and its language a complicated one.
Needless to say, an experienced stenographer was a necessary part of these Ouija sessions. Patience sometimes worked
on as many as four novels at once, spelling a few sentences
for one, then a few lines for another, throwing in a poem
here and there and occasionally stopping to enter into conversation with the Ouija sitters. She never lost her place as
we would, but could pick up any story just where she had
left it. She also became well known for her impromptu
poems, composed on the spot from topics or images suggested by onlookers at the Ouija session. My favorite of
these short poems is a response to a request for a children's
bedtime prayer more appropriate than the insipid and often
morbid ones common to the day. I grew up with the lines
"If I should die before I wake, I pray the Lord my soul to
take" echoing around me as I went to sleep, and even as a
child I considered this unnecessarily grim. Patience Worth's
offering:

> *I, Thy child forever, play*
> *About Thy knees at close of day;*
> *Within Thy arms I now shall creep*
> *And learn Thy wisdom while I sleep.*

Since samples of Patience Worth's peculiar archaic style of speech appear at the beginnings of both this chapter and Chapter Two, I'll include here an excerpt from her only long message in modern prose, the novel *Hope Trueblood*. This passage comes near the beginning of the tale, setting its scene and introducing characters and leaving us tantalized, wondering what comes next. (Though *Hope Trueblood* has been out of print many years, it can still be found in public libraries old enough to have ordered it at the height of its popularity—1918.)

"The man should be held up before the people. He is clothed in the garb of the hypocrite." I sucked the plum stone and wondered what a hypocrite was and if they were upon the road at night. "Sally Trueblood's brat!" I looked to the sampler and read slowly, "God is Love." And I wondered what a brat was.

Mr. Passwater seemed not to relish his port, and Miss Patricia sipped hers gingerly. I sneezed and Miss Patricia seemed not to hear me, but continued, " 'Tis shameful."

I got from off the hassock and tiptoed over to the castle beneath the glass and stood rapt. Beside it lay a book of prayer. It was thin and flat and black, and I knew it was Miss Patricia's. From this I went up to the what-all, and the lights played o'er it and I stood before it filled with wonder. Upon the third shelf was a china dog, with a babe upon its back. Oh, to touch this! I turned stealthily and looked to Miss Patricia. She did not see. I reached forth one hand and tiptoed and it was mine. I hugged it close to make sure and the what-all shook and rattled. Miss Patricia was upon her feet in an instant and pounced upon me, taking me within her grasp so suddenly that I let fall the china dog. Miss Patricia gasped:

"A thief! My dear brother William's pet! Oh, that the earth should be so sinful! Reuben Passwater, take this brat out of this house! Shut her out!"

And Miss Patricia shook me. I whimpered, and stooped to

pick up the dog, tenderly, leaving my tears to fall upon
it, and offered it to her hand sniffling. Miss Patricia took
it and placed it upon the third shelf where it had stood
and I backed away staring, my fingers within my mouth
and the tears coursing down my cheeks. I knew what a
thief was. Miss Patricia stared at me and looked at my feet,
crying out:

"Why does your worthless mother leave you free in
night's hour to visit Christian homes? Your feet are upon
the ground. Where are your better shoes?"

"I haven't none, thanks. She has promised 'em at Mayin'."

This seemed to send Miss Patricia into a storm, for she
rocked and shrieked and beat her bosom, crying out that
the tongues of the village were lashes and that no Christian
might dwell among them, stopping only to shout: "Take
her away! Take her away!"

Mr. Passwater stooped slowly and took up a shoe and
put it on, then the other just as slowly. He arose and
buttoned his vest, sighed, went for his greatcoat and made
a sign for me to follow. We went out of a narrow hallway
that smelled of mutton. Mr. Passwater opened the latch
and we stepped into the night. I followed him, frightened,
and he did not speak. I did not seem to fear Mr. Passwater,
but the dark. He seemed silent, and, as I write, I see his
dark form stooped and hear him step heavily and my light
footfall following, pattering.

During Patience Worth's years of public notice, the mystery of her identity remained a foremost topic of debate.
Patience herself had very little interest in the subject, insisting that the importance of her messages lay in the words
themselves. She gave few and sketchy details of her supposed lifetime as "Patience Worth," and these she revealed
only in the context of her poetry and stories. (For instance,
she seemed to know the countryside of southern England,
she never married, she sailed to North America near the
end of her life.) The philosophy and opinions of this extraordinary voice of Ouija were likewise tucked neatly away

in her literary productions, and can't be extracted and sum-marized with their grace and wit intact. That is as Patience Worth intended, so I'll leave her here and go on to other voices. For readers who want to know more of Patience, there are, besides the works I've already mentioned, two books *about* Patience Worth, both out of print but avail-able at libraries: *Patience Worth: A Psychic Mystery*, by Casper Yost (Henry Holt and Co., 1916), and *The Case of Patience Worth*, by Walter Franklin Prince (University Books, 1964—first published in 1927 by the Boston Society for Psychic Research).

A Ouija experience similar in form to Pearl Curran's adventure with Patience Worth is recounted in the anony-mously written book of 1920, mentioned earlier, called *Our Unseen Guest*. The authors, a married couple known to us only as "Darby" and "Joan," unexpectedly made the ac-quaintance of a voice of Ouija they called Stephen. Like Patience, Stephen presents himself as a very definite per-sonality, complete with a life history that is mentioned but not emphasized, as well as the more convincing evidence of individuality shown in peculiarities of speech. Like Pa-tience, Stephen claims to be able to communicate because he is specially "atuned" to one Ouija partner (Joan). The messages Stephen and Patience bring have many similarities at their most basic levels of meaning (we'll consider these in Chapter Nine). The styles of the two, however, are worlds apart, just as Pearl Curran and Joan must have been very different people.

From the meager clues Darby lets fall in *Our Unseen Guest*, we can deduce that Joan and Darby were both col-lege educated and that they both held professional jobs in a large city (Chicago, I've since discovered). Darby's ac-count of their Ouija beginnings shows the couple's articu-lacy and, compared with Pearl Curran, their sophistication as well:

> Our first experience with psychic phenomena occurred
> on the evening of December 7, 1916—by way of a Ouija

board. Neither Joan nor I had ever seen a Ouija board before. The "toy" came into our hands quite by accident.

We were taking our dinners at a private boarding-house some blocks from the apartment building in which we lived. On the evening in question a sudden storm blew off the lake, while we were at table, and after the meal Joan and I wandered into a deserted sitting-room to wait until the wind and sleet abated. There one of the residents had left the Ouija, a remnant doubtless of some Hallowe'en party.

"How does the thing work?" Joan asked.

I read the directions; we rested the board, whereon the alphabet was printed in two semi-circles, upon our knees, and put the tips of our fingers on the flatiron-like pointer.

"Now," said I, "this tripod affair is supposed to move from letter to letter, spelling out a message."

Thus we sat for a period—ten minutes, perhaps. We joked, I remember, of the good fortunes Ouija would tell us. But no message came. Then, just as we were about to give up, the tripod began to move.

"Quality of consciousness," it spelled. A pause—then, once more, "Quality of consciousness."

"Darby!" Joan took her fingers from the pointer. "You can't fool me like that. You did it! 'Quality of consciousness'—that doesn't mean anything, anyway."

I looked into Joan's eyes. Was it she who had moved the tripod, or did she honestly accuse me?

"Not guilty!" I pleaded. For a moment we faced each other in silence. Then said Joan, gravely, "Let's try it again." So we tried it again.

On the instant the tripod gathered strength. Over the alphabet it moved, slowly, yet with machine-like precision, pausing on this letter and that. Here are the words it spelled:

"For you two I have a message, a revelation. Communication is so slow, so difficult, that I can do little more than give you the suggestion. But if you will reason along the lines I point out, you can reach the truth."

"What truth?"

"In as far," the answer came, "as it is given you to understand, that ultimate truth—the why, the whence, the whither—which men have longed to know since knowledge was."

As you can see, these are direct and purposeful people, conversing with a Ouija voice of similar temperament. No Patience for poetry and allusion here—just plain revelation. It is a complex revelation that emerges, though, a philosophy that brings the worlds on both sides of death into a hopeful and communicative alliance. Stephen builds this philosophy through many lessons, defining new terms as he goes and stretching Darby's and Joan's understanding with each Ouija session. We'll listen in on one of the earlier conversations, feeling the intimations of possibilities yet to unfold.

"Define the quality and quantity of consciousness," I said.

Stephen answered: "Quality is soul, as when you say a person has a beautiful or sensitive soul. Soul is the best word for our present purpose, though character would in a measure express the thought. I have told you that graduated consciousness is, in part, reborn into your world. I tell you now that the part so reborn is the quality, the soul."

"Your definition," I said, "is not as opaque as a brick wall, nor is it as clear as a windowpane."

"Later the thought will shape itself," Stephen assured me. "And now for quantity. Quantity is that development which results from the use an individual makes of his quality of consciousness."

"Do you mean growth of character?" asked Joan.

"Exactly," Stephen replied.

"When I speak of the quality of gold as being distinct from the quality of iron, the word presents no difficulty. Yet when I speak of the quality of human consciousness you are confused. This should not be, but—as Joan might say—because it is, I tell you the quality of a man's consciousness is his soul.

"Take electricity. It is force. Take gravitation. It, too, is force. Now the thing that distinguishes these two forces one from the other is their differing quality.

"Well, the quality of human consciousness is parallel to the quality of gravitation and to the quality of electricity. The earth term heretofore used for the quality of human consciousness has been soul, by which term men have sought to name that which distinguishes them from all else. In other words, they have recognized the distinctiveness of their own quality."

"Why, that's simple enough," I was forced to admit.

"And all great truths are most astounding in their simplicity," spelled the Ouija board.

"Take electricity again. Can you not see that its quality is fixed? It is that very unalterableness of quality that makes it electricity rather than, for example, centrifugal force. So it is with human consciousness. But now get this: Though your quality on the earth-plane is restricted, I on my plane am free to develop quality, just as you now are free to develop quantity."

The tripod paused, then moved, then halted again, then said: "Does it mean anything to you when I say that the only difference between your plane of consciousness and mine is that yours is quantitative in its development, while mine is qualitative? At any rate, from now on I shall speak of my plane as the qualitative plane and yours as the quantitative."

Stephen never claimed sole authorship of this message; in fact he paused in his Ouija board delivery at times to consult other personalities accessible to his range of being. One of these "spirits" became so enthusiastically involved in the revelation that he sometimes overruled Stephen's control of the Ouija board and spelled out words himself. Darby and Joan learned to recognize the arrival of this other personality even before any words were spelled, by the sudden difference in the feel of the pointer under their fingers. Darby hints broadly that he and Joan guessed the identity of this messenger, whom they nicknamed "the professor." In terms even more vague, lest he be accused of quackery or Ouija board egotism, Darby intimates that the professor may be philosopher William James. Whatever his identity, the professor is a delightful Ouija voice with a decidedly didactic style. Here he is, lecturing on one of his favorite topics:

> The free will of man, my dear sir, is the one attribute that is wholly and distinctly his own. Degrees of consciousness nearing man have something that approaches reason, something even closer to memory, and are possessed of attributes comparable to the five senses. But animal life does not have free will. This is man's peculiar possession. Because of free will man is man.
>
> The will of man is hampered not even by his quality, be it low. It is as free for all men as for one. But for an individual to live up to his quality he must use his will in the gathering of quantity. Not to use the freedom of one's will is to deny one's self of self. Free will constitutes every man's opportunity, permitting him to control the degree of consciousness he attains on graduation.
>
> Do not make any mistake about the freedom of man's will. It is his to use, and use develops it, just as exercise develops the muscles of one's body. Disuse deadens it. And as to the purpose of free will make no mistake. For it is only as the free will carries out the behests of that still, small voice, man's quality of consciousness, that the lessons of earth are finished, the book closed, and a wider world, a greater freedom and more perfect understanding attained upon graduation.

Not all voices of Ouija present themselves in such individualized fashion. My belief is that we tend to receive

messages in whatever form we find easiest to digest. For
many people, conversation with a specific "spirit" feels
more comfortable than messages from "the void." For others
the reverse is true. In 1919 Betty and Stewart White began
to receive Ouija messages from a source identified to them
only as "the Invisibles." Ouija words spelled out lessons in
spiritual and psychic development, practical day-by-day
lessons that Stewart White, a successful writer already, incorporated into a series of books. The first volumes of Ouija
lessons, published in 1925 and 1928, made no mention of
the source of Stewart's inspiration, but in 1937, when finally
he felt that he could make public such an odd source of
knowledge without feeling foolish or being called a fool,
Stewart White produced *The Betty Book*, in which he gave
all the details of the long adventure and quoted long passages straight from the spirits as well. Here is a sample of
the guidance of "the Invisibles":

> Walk through your days as a creature with folded
> wings, conscious of the possession of another element and
> the ability to enter it. When worries and world annoyances
> come, you can rise strongly and determinedly, spend a few
> moments in calm, and at once descend reinforced to the
> object in hand.
>
> If you want to get anywhere, you have to take this
> philosophy home with you, and dress it, and eat it, and
> breathe it, and motor down town with it. When you are
> able to do that you are ready for something more. At
> present anything more than what you have would over-
> flow into merely an intellectual appreciation.
>
> Months of successful effort must elapse, until you are
> steeped, saturated, permeated with the fluid strength of
> spiritual contact. At first you are struggling in a kind of
> blind instinct to gather strength, but without being able
> to see what you have achieved. Keep your faith in the
> vitality of effort. It requires mastering before you can feel
> the repose, the assurance of strength and progress.

You must have something to which to refer yourself: first as a stake in water swirling about; then as planted in sand; and then as a fixed point in space. It doesn't matter how you symbolize it, but *you must have something constant in yourself.*

Very often my results with the Ouija board have had a tone similar to "the Invisibles' "—soothing paragraphs of encouragement and advice, delivered from a very vaguely identified source. When I began my Ouija explorations I would have scoffed loudly, and felt fearful underneath the scoff, at the idea of "spirit communicators." I've since loosened my grip on that fear and had some lovely Ouija conversations with Ouija voices full of personality and history, but the less specific voices remain the most constant form at my board. Here are two examples of guiding messages from my notes. My friend Laurel accompanied me in these productions, and the advice was meant for us both, though sometimes more especially for one or the other. For these messages, we sat down at the Ouija board in the morning and asked for thoughts to take with us through the day.

Place your trust in the infinite flow of your destiny. Your fate is to grow in love and wisdom. Do not fight it as if without your worries fate would take you to loneliness and despair. Let go of the arrogance of thinking you are alone in this world without spiritual guides. Angels hover near you and you say, "I am alone. No one cares about me. I must make sense of the world myself."

You are both more and less important than that. More because you are watched and guided carefully when you allow. Angels cry when you do. Less because you are presently in a limited situation from which you cannot possibly figure out on your own the world's or your life's meaning. You need spiritual guidance and we need you just as surely. Let these words permeate your beings today.

—January 17, 1977

Love. Move in love and needs will take care of themselves. Move in joy and fear will run past you quickly.
You are alive and there is joy and thankfulness to be found
in that if you will allow it to enter you. Move in love and
joy and the need for what you call security will fade from
you. This security is not the basic necessity you think it is.
Your real security lies in the eternally growing wisdom
and joy of your beings. The physical and emotional security you value is necessary to you only because you do
not see your real and lasting security. You can only become aware of your eternal beings as you take away your
attention from false security. This does not mean that you
must become beggars in the streets, just that you must
turn your attention to love.   —January 23, 1977

We've looked at literature and philosophy as produced
by personalitied voices of Ouija, and at inspirational advice
from undefined sources. Now it's time to remind ourselves
of two important points. One, that when we speak of the
"source" of a voice of Ouija being a spirit or a vague force
or an anything else, we're indulging in a convenient conven-
tion. Whatever Patience Worth may be, for instance, she
is a much more complex phenomenon than our image of a
disembodied spinster poet transported from seventeenth
century England. Whatever she is, Patience does not exist
as we know her apart from Pearl Curran. Perhaps there is
another Patience Worth in some otherworldly dimension
of experience, but in our world Pearl Curran has *created*,
not with conscious effort but simply by living her life, the
only Patience Worth there is. In the same way, just by
bringing our unique perspectives and histories to the Ouija
board, each of us creates there some confluence of words
and meanings never before seen in this world.

Which brings us to the second point to remember: the
sampling of voices of Ouija in this chapter is just that.
We've held up particular pieces of the Ouija patchwork
quilt. They are meant to delight and inspire us. They are

not intended as a description of possibilities. In the same way you might see that a neighbor brought a red calico square to the quilting bee and Aunt Minnie brought a purple striped piece, and you might like the red print and learn a new appliqué stitch from Aunt Minnie's contribution to the quilt, and still *not* jump to the conclusion that quilts can be made two ways, from red squares or from purple squares, *just so* can we see that voices of Ouija here are either very personified or very vague *and* there must be many other colors we can use as well.

I'll say this another way, with one more example from my own Ouija adventures. My current Ouija preoccupation began one afternoon when Laurel and I sat down at the board and said to it: "Write a novel." The pointer started right in, surprising us both immensely. The surprise has deepened since, as we unroll complicated plots and subplots, as separate characters and strands of story finally meet each other, as mysteries are solved and darker mysteries created. There seems to be no single Ouija personality in charge of the production, though from time to time the story is told by an unnamed and invisible narrator. At other times various characters tell their corners of the story, each with a distinct vocabulary and tone. Here is the beginning of the tale:

> Just now we're questioning no one, though since Jeremy asked why not I've begun wondering myself. Of course I wouldn't say it out loud. Neither would Jeremy if he wasn't such a new one. Not that I could tell you why—it's that oddness I feel sometimes, like the day Mary Ellen went away. It was announced on the box at lunch hour that Mary Ellen had been promoted, because of her good will, unflinching faithfulness, and all those other good qualities they always describe at such announcements, to a post in the laundry at All-in-one. The box said she left Tuesday evening to join the shirt-press staff as they prepared for the coming summer solstice banquet. Now I'm

sure it's not sour grapes I feel—some of the girls here go
out for shirt-pleat awards, but I'm not one of them. I just
don't have ambitions about ironing in the capital, though
I'm as good a worker as any of them, when it comes down
to it. And I don't feel bad that Mary Ellen didn't come and
say goodbye to me, though I confess I would have expected her to. I guessed she was just too pressed for time—
oh the stupid puns you pick up at the laundry works—if
I changed my occupation everyone would know me as a
presser still. But how likely is a change that drastic? Such
odd ideas springing on me lately and I don't know why.
But this other oddness—how my mind wanders when I try
writing a simple bit of the day before I sleep, wanting I
guess to distinguish each day somehow from the others.
Anyway, I've had this queasy feeling all week, since Mary
Ellen left, and I don't know what it is or how to describe
it except to say it's the same feeling I got this afternoon
when Jeremy asked why don't we ask questions anymore.
There's some connection—or maybe it's just the change
of life affecting my nerves. I even thought, today, of sending a letter to Mary Ellen in All-in-one, and I started
writing it in my mind as I changed the press, when all at
once I realized—letters can't go from Fernville to All-in-
one. Letters are only delivered within the towns. It's always
been this way and all our news and communication with
All-in-one and everywhere comes from the box and that's
the way it always has been and should be. Still I do wish
Jeremy and Mary Ellen both would get out of my
thoughts. I remember, and not so long ago, when I didn't
have a care in the world, and everything meant just what
it seemed to. Well, I sure won't go saying any of this confusion anywhere but this little notebook. They'll never
have to return me to Eden because of early senility.

From here the tale shifts to other voices and very different perspectives, following the activities of a group of
people, Jeremy and Mary Ellen among them, engaged in

clandestine cultivation of psychic powers. Occasionally Shirley the laundry worker's diary brings in a counterpointed perspective: she knows Mary Ellen and Jeremy of the psychic circle only through their jobs at the laundry, but she is drawn to them, and writes about them, perhaps because she is just beginning to question "official" reality, to feel odd, at odds with it, and she senses that for these two everything does not mean just what it seems to mean. The "official" reality, revealed in Shirley's first diary entry only by oblique clues—the "box," her vague fears about feeling odd, the reference to being returned to Eden—continues to unfold slowly, clue by clue, through the action of the story and the words of the participants.

Each character in this drama seems wholly an individual, a fully functioning, unique Ouija personality. Their interaction appears to be as complex as any between embodied people. The timing and coordination of the whole production is intelligently and creatively planned *somewhere*. Where? Who? How? That's what we'll explore next.

CHAPTER EIGHT

How the Ouija®
Board Works

*The superstition of the past is the science of
the present, the proverb of the future.*

—STEWART EDWARD WHITE, 1937

We can begin to ask this chapter's question by studying
the details of Ouija's movements, piecing together the findings of many careful observers and seeing what sort of
larger whole those observations describe. By the end of the
chapter we will have gone as far into the absolute as present
scientific fact can take us, still without *quite* answering our
question about how this small toy works. To complete our
understanding, we must ask our question again in Chapter
Nine, this time from the opposite end of the spectrum,
starting with theories about how the universe works and
filtering slowly down to our alphabets and pointers. Only
when we have followed both these directions, *and* woven
together their separate strands of fact and conjecture, will
we be able to see what a complex shimmering sturdy garment we're wearing—even though we've been wearing it
all our lives.

To start with the most purely mechanical aspect of our question: how does the pointer actually move? The simplest part of the answer—we push it with our fingers—is obvious only to someone who has never tried the device. For the rest of us, "the hand is quicker than the eye" has taken on new meaning, for we have to admit that our own hands are in this case quicker than our own eyes. The muscles of our fingers are able to exert pressures so subtle and precise that even though we give the process our full attention, we can't consciously detect that we push the pointer of Ouija. (If you *can* feel your fingers pushing, lighten up.)

Forces more mysterious than muscles can play a part in the pointer's movements too, in fact *may* create some part of all Ouija movement. I've seen a pointer continue to make its way across the alphabet *after* both partners had taken their fingers away. Friends of mine report Ouija pointers flying out from under their fingers to sail across the room. You may have noticed by now that at some sessions the pointer seems especially "charged" somehow with energy. It may almost vibrate under your fingertips, or move about with such force that you feel the pointer's blast-off into outer space may be imminent. All these occurrences, which in scientific terms would be called examples of psychokinesis, imply that some type of energy other than simple muscle power has collected in the pointer. The properties and behavior of this energy are hot subjects of debate among present-day researchers of the paranormal, as we shall see.

The most intriguing way to view our question is to wonder not only how the pointer moves, but how it comes to spell out messages so far removed from our conscious knowledge. Both the unexplained physical movements of the pointer and the transmission of information through the device can be imagined as dependent on the same mysterious energy source. This is the hypothesis, or working guess, of many psychic researchers today. The Ouija board can provide us, as we've already seen, with examples from almost the entire range of psychic phenomena: telepathy (communicating from mind to mind), clairvoyance (seeing objects or events not visually accessible), precognition (foretelling the future), psychokinesis (physical effects such as Ouija pointer movement from apparently nonphysical sources), and survival phenomena (apparent evidence of life after death). Since these areas overlap and reinforce each other abundantly, and in fact are altogether tangled, we'll leave them that way, as others before us have done. We'll follow the whole knotted tangle down the path of recent scientific research, assuming that where one strand leads we are bound to find the others too.

It will come as no surprise to us to learn that the Ouija board itself has never been scientifically tested. The toy not only has the sort of reputation that can make a scientist shiver in his test tubes, it also has the distinction of implicating so many factors in its behavior that tracing back to the source becomes far too complicated a task. Luckily for us, simpler tools utilizing the same principles as Ouija *have* been studied in controlled settings, and we can reflect the results back on our own endeavor. We'll do well to remember that though we're moving into the domain of science, these areas still lead an uncertain existence on the outer fringes of that exacting land. Even today many established and respected scientists deny that any of the unexplained phenomena we're examining exist at all. Meanwhile we will look in on the work of the *second generation* of psychic researchers, who carry on in spite of their invisibility in the scientific establishment.

The Ouija board is a refined and rather complicated version of a range of tools that utilize the human nervous system's talents as a receiver and translator of information. The necessary ingredients are (1) a human consciousness with which to ask a question or focus in on a particular topic, (2) a nervous system (this includes our brains as well as every nerve in our bodies) capable of scanning the available information environment, selecting an "answer," translating that answer into language meaningful to the conscious mind of the questioner, and transmitting the chosen information via (3) a device that amplifies subconscious motor movements and/or utilizes some other, as yet unknown, form of energy generated or conducted by the human body.

The board's particular richness lies in its interweaving of *two* human beings as receivers and transmitters and creators of its messages, and also in the wide spectrum of reply provided by the alphabet and numerals. The planchette has the added advantage of the language of lines; its pencil-pointer can draw pictures or diagrams. Dowsing tools, which range from simple forked sticks to professional-looking metal rods, work within a basic language of yes and no, with refinements, such as indications of direction or depth, invented by individual dowsers. The simplest tool of all is the pendulum, just a hand-held string with a weight tied to it. The pendulum is another yes-and-no indicator, swinging back and forth or describing circles to make its replies.

The pendulum and dowsing rod are the tools similar to Ouija best suited to scientific scrutiny, since the simplicity of their mechanisms and their narrow range of possible reply rule out many of the board's confusions and allow the experimenters to control more aspects of their adventure. Dowsing (this term can refer to use of a pendulum as well as dowsing rods) has the added advantage of a long history of use outside the parameters of "the occult." This makes it much more attractive to scientists, and less scary. We've all heard of the old practice of dowsing for underground water, in which the dowser walks along holding the ends of a forked stick before him in both hands, and the stick points down when underground water is crossed. This method for finding water is widely accepted today in much of Europe, and widely used, although not so well accepted, in the U.S.

Dowsing for water is the most mundane and easily explained application of our range of supersensory tools. Underground water has been shown to create a weak electromagnetic field. It is a simple step to assume that the instruments that are our bodies can detect such fields, just as our bodies react to changes in the gravitational field caused by the moon's rotation about the earth. Dowsing only begins with such simplicities as water-witching, however. In the Soviet Union, dowsing has evolved into a highly respected and "scientific" activity called "the biophysical method." Russian dowsers, traveling via cross-country motor vehicles, search for every sort of underground treasure, from copper ore to buried archeological sites. The Russians' report on conditions affecting dowsing ability could easily be mistaken for Hester Travers Smith expounding on conditions affecting Ouija board operation: both say illness, cold winds, bad moods, and negative or idiotic remarks or questions from casual observers detrimentally affect the endeavor.

Dowsing enters the medical domain on a large scale in France, where the use of the pendulum to diagnose illness has been given the name "radiesthesia." The practice is so widespread that French medical dowsers even have a union —*Syndicat National des Radiesthésistes*. Many of these practitioners use the pendulum to prescribe medications as well as in diagnosis. One of the most famous (or infamous, depending on one's vantage point) of French medical dowsers is the Reverend Père Jean Jurion, a Catholic priest who uses a pendulum to diagnose illness and to prescribe homeopathic medications. Rev. Jurion has been taken to court by the French government countless times for his unorthodox, unschooled and unlicensed medical practices. The most encouraging sign of progress we can note in his story is that the Catholic Church continues to support Rev. Jurion. French Catholic monasteries and nunneries were Europe's surfacing ground for the planchette over a hundred years ago. Church authorities at that time forbade use of the planchette, but here it is in another form, focused now on medicine rather than metaphysics, and this time used with the Church's blessing.

In this country medical dowsing began with a characteristically American emphasis on technology. Early this century, San Francisco doctor Albert Abrams developed diagnostic machines with complicated electronic circuitry, on the hypothesis that all living organisms give out characteristic "electronic emanations." His machines were meant to "read" these emanations, which varied with the patient's state of health. Abrams had the good fortune of being independently wealthy as well as being a respected and well-trained medical doctor. His most inventive pupil, Ruth Drown, had neither of these assets; she was denounced as a quack and lived out the last years of her life in the California Institute for Women, the only women's prison in the state of California. It's easy enough to imagine, from Ruth Drown's startling work, how she attracted such intense opposition. After spending several years modifying Albert Abrams' electronic gadgetry, discarding many of the parts considered essential and finding that the devices still worked, Ruth Drown went on to initiate the long-distance diagnosis of patients, working from just a blood sample or even a lock of hair. Next she found that by placing a lock of a patient's hair or a blood sample in her apparatus along with a photographic plate, she could obtain photographs of the *entire patient*, with internal organs outlined and problem areas clearly visible. She diagnosed hundreds of patients by this method without ever meeting the individuals personally.

Although all of Ruth Drown's equipment was destroyed by the government, other researchers have since replicated her findings, sometimes without having known of her work at all—even the mysterious photographic process has been reclaimed. The field has taken on a new seriousness with the widespread adoption of the title "radionics." Edward Russell, the most knowledgeable writer in this area, defines radionics well:

Radionics, a word coined about 1935, is the modern name for an ancient medical art. It is based on the fact that the

human mind can be attuned to detect characteristic emanations from all forms of organic or inorganic matter.
Radionics—usually assisted by instruments to help focus
the mind of the operator—uses the superconscious mind
to diagnose and treat diseases in humans, animals, and
crops.

Here we've come to the confession that the purpose of
radionic instruments is to "help focus the mind of the operator." In this field, scientific progress has led to more and
more *simplified* technology. Ruth Drown began the process
by discarding unnecessary components of Abrams' diagnostic machines. Other investigators went further. John
Campbell, independent scientist and editor of the science-
fiction magazine *Analog*, found that the devices worked
just as well when they were not plugged in to their electric
power source. He went on to make the surprising discovery
that a penciled diagram of the circuitry could replace the
actual apparatus. Scientific research has brought us back to
the simplicity of the Ouija board or pendulum as the most
elegant and appropriate tool for our venture. Science begins
to echo what I've said in various ways throughout this
book: *we* are the essential ingredients at the Ouija board;
our minds and bodies are inconceivably intricate instruments
capable of receiving and translating information from other
human beings, from other animal species, from the plant
and mineral worlds, and perhaps from "emanations" that
originate in other-than-physical realities too.

I've skipped over innumerable examples of research in
this large soup that goes by so many names—radionics,
dowsing, radiesthesia, the biophysical method. There are
even entire terminologies I've left out, along with their
creators and the important work they've done—psycho-
tronics, paraphysics, psychoenergetics—we may hear from
some of them yet. For those of you interested in learning
more about recent and current scientific work in this field,
I recommend *Future Science* (an anthology edited by John

White and Stanley Krippner, an Anchor Press/Doubleday paperback, 1977) as a good beginning. In these pages we'll have to let many verifying examples go by unannounced in order to continue on the trail of our elusive question. Just how does Ouija work, anyway?

Only recently has the equivalent of our question begun to be asked among researchers in paranormal fields. The first generation of psychic researchers concentrated on finding ways to show that this bundle of unexplained phenomena did indeed exist. For a while researchers were stymied by the scientific establishment's insistence on duplicative tests—experiments anyone else could repeat and emerge with exactly the same results as those for the original experiment. Very gradually this criterion has faded in importance. Scientists have begun to accept the fact, obvious to most nonscientists, that the experimenter's unique and never-quite-repeatable personality and attitude *always* affect the course of any experiment. When the experiment is one in which the researcher's mind and nervous system are the primary sensing instruments and raw material, there is no longer any sense in talking of "replicating the experiment."

The current paranormal researchers, the second generation, realize that "it is the duty of Science to wait upon Nature, to reverently listen to what she chooses to tell, and in the way it pleases her to utter it," as scientist and psychic investigator Epes Sargent declared in 1868. Paranormal research is at a stage analogous to the beginning of electricity's development, at which time Thomas Edison was asked "What is electricity?" He replied, "I don't know, but it works."

Speculation runs wild and free with regard to the nature of the energy that spells Ouija words, or allows telepathy, or creates a photograph of a cow from a sample of the cow's blood. That it is the same energy we seek in all these unexplained phenomena is fairly well agreed upon among psychic researchers. Whether this mysterious energy is actually a physical, measurable substance, however, makes a great argument with no conclusive evidence currently available.

Many of today's paranormal researchers are involved in a search for the "substance" of this energy, an attempt to show its physicality. They are encouraged by long centuries of such a force's recognition in cultural traditions the world over: "prana" in India and Tibet, "ch'i" in China and "ki" in Japan, the "astral light" of European magic, the "etheric force" of spiritualism. Several eccentric researchers of the last century have independently "discovered" this force also, adding the confusion of their separate terminologies and the controversy over their work to the general hubbub. Wilhelm Reich, another inventor who died in a U.S. prison while serving a fraud conviction, is today the best known of these researchers; his name for the energy whose trail we follow is "orgone." Baron Karl von Reichenbach, with his "odic force," is another researcher whose conceptualization of the unknown energy is still discussed today.

We can compare the descriptions of prana, ch'i, orgone, all the ways our mystery "substance" has been defined, and next to these descriptions we can place the results of all the recent scientific tests for this energy. What characteristics hold true for every description? Surprisingly, quite a detailed list can be made, though still without giving us the identity of a physical substance or process responsible for paranormal phenomena. Six of the characteristics of this force are:

1. It is associated with every animal, plant and mineral body, and also is observed to be present in the operation of electricity, light, magnetism and chemical reactions, though it cannot be defined by any of these processes or phenomena.

2. Any complex organic structure (for instance, human beings, plants, crystals, planets) contains a series of geometrically arranged points at which this energy is highly concentrated (acupuncture points and chakras are ways of

describing these points in people; "ley lines" or power points are examples on the earth's surface).

3. This substance or energy is everywhere, permeating every object and filling all space; it is absorbed by organic material and refracted by metals.

4. In the religious and occult traditions, this energy is said to create matter and life; scientific studies have only gone so far as to observe that changes in this energy surrounding living organisms *precede* changes in the organism itself (for instance, an influx of the energy precedes a healing event; before physical death the energy departs).

5. The energy flows between living organisms and objects, creating "threads" of energy that continue to link objects (and people) once in any way connected. In occult traditions it is said that we control these threads of energy through our thoughts and emotions. In scientific study, this energy flow can be implied in examples of telepathic communication. It is more dramatically shown in the well-known studies involving the sensitivity and "feelings" of plants, or in the field of agricultural radionics, where crops are treated for insect pests or encouraged to grow by workers who are hundreds or thousands of miles from the plants, by using only a leaf or an aerial photograph of the area to be treated. (The practice of agricultural radionics has been so successful that it is in a temporary state of suspension in this country, after having been squelched twenty-five years ago by the pesticide and fertilizer branch of the oil industry.)

6. This energy can be visually observed under certain conditions: directly, by people who learn to move their own states of consciousness to a vantage point from which the energy becomes visible, or by means of special lenses or the photographic technique known as "Kirlian photography."

Though we still have no concrete definition of the nature and workings of this mysterious all-pervasive energy, there are additional hints we can gather through the workings of processes that *can* be explained and measured by present-day scientists. One of the most intriguing of these is the phenomenon of electrostatic fields, first announced in the 1930's by Dr. Harold Saxton Burr of Yale University. Burr found that by using extremely sensitive voltmeters he could measure electrostatic fields surrounding every sort of living organism—people, trees, salamanders, even slime molds. These "L fields," as he called them ("L" for Life), show many of the same characteristics I've just listed for our formative force. Most importantly, the fields register changes in well-being before physical changes become manifest. Burr believed these fields to be the actual formative energy of the universe, the unknown force we seek. He called his finding "the electrodynamic theory of life," and with his colleague Dr. F. S. C. Northrop and his pupil Dr. Leonard J. Ravitz, Jr., Burr studied electrostatic fields for forty years, 'til his death in 1973. His work has received little attention from scientists, perhaps because of the grandiosity of the theoretical claims Burr attached to his findings. It's interesting to note that Wilhelm Reich also came to the conclusion that electrostatic energy is a manifestation of the ultimate formative force of the universe; Reich claimed that static electricity was not really electricity at all, but orgone. Most of today's paranormal researchers currently consider the phenomenon of electrostatic fields to be an indicator or correlate of "the unknown energy," something that occurs *with* this formative force and is perhaps one aspect of it.

Another valuable hint is contained in the recent research of three Columbia University physicists (I. I. Rabi, P. Kusch and S. Millman), who constructed an apparatus with which they were able to show that every molecule of any sort functions as a radio transmitter and receiver, continuously broadcasting, with waves varying in length over the whole range of the electromagnetic spectrum and beyond. Each molecule has a vocabulary of over a million different wavelengths. This discovery brings with it some of the widest implications we've seen so far in our search, just because it *doesn't* involve any mysterious or controversial form of energy, but instead pushes processes with which we are already familiar into mind-boggling extensions.

As we sit at our talking boards, we find that communication of information, coming to us by means other than our five senses and resulting in words spelled out by this simple contraption, has become suddenly an easy process to imagine. As possible avenues of converse we now have:

1. The sensitivity of our bodies to gravitational and electromagnetic changes.

2. The interaction of our electrostatic field with other electrostatic fields (including the field of our planet, which, yes, does have its own field, extending from the ground to an altitude of about sixty miles, all the way around the earth).

3. Cellular and molecular communication within our bodies.

4. Long-range radio signals picked up, amplified and translated by the molecules of our bodies.

5. Communication over any distance through the medium of the formative energy of the universe, that fills all space and is absorbed by our bodies. This information may travel along "threads" of denser energy created by our thoughts (our questions to Ouija) and connecting us with sources of information.

6. What will probably be found to be most common, *combinations* of all these different processes. It has already been shown, for instance, that many environmental communications (gravitational changes, sunspots, atmospheric disturbances) are received first by the electrostatic field and then passed on to the physical organism. Perhaps a complex series of translations of information always takes place, from subtler, less physical forms to more solid, from faster and more complex to simple and slow. Certainly the words of a pointer seem plodding and limited when we see them beside a single molecule with a million wavelength vocabulary or a not-quite-physical substance connecting

everything in the universe. Just here lies the wonder of our Ouija endeavor—that, though slow and very limited beings we may be, we are connected somehow with the mysterious immensities of the universe around us, and not blindly connected but given the potential to actually *know* this universe, to converse with it and so learn who we are.

Not every scientist in the paranormal field is on the trail of a physical form for the connective energy of the universe. Some, including the granddaddy of ESP research, J. B. Rhine of Duke University, believe that the energy research we've described but have not been able to capture is not physical at all and will never be adequately defined in physical terms. Other scientists recognize that even if we do isolate and name such a physical force we will by no means have come to the end of our search. When electricity was defined and harnessed, many questions were answered and many practical possibilities opened up to us, but most important, the limits of our abilities to perceive the universe were pushed back into a wider circle, thus expanding our view of *what is* and at the same time providing us with a new, more subtle and profound set of limits.

The unraveling of atomic structure provided the same sort of redefinition both of the reality we know *and* of the universe outside our understanding. Just so, our beginning knowledge of electrostatic fields, or of molecular radio communication, can potentially make great broadenings in the circle of our species' "reality," facing us with a correspondingly greater circumference of "unknown." Proof of the existence of the unknown energy with so many names would likewise explain much to us that has remained hidden through countless discoveries of slower, more easily observed processes. And then we would also face a new, larger unknown.

William Tiller is a Stanford University professor with an unusually broad and knowledgeable perspective on the progress of both paranormal research and modern physics. He visualizes a universe that manifests itself in a series of processes ranging from the dense and mechanical, through the finer and more exacting realm of chemical reactions, on through the range of electric, magnetic and gravitational phenomena, through the media in which our "formative energy" may occur, by way of what Tiller calls "nonphysical space–time fields," where space and time are creative changing forces rather than the stable givens as in our currently perceived world. Finally, his vision encompasses the domain of pure mind—energy with all understanding and all possibility before it. Dr. Tiller says:

> In our very distant future, we are likely to find that there is only *one* energy which has manifold expressions depending on the state of consciousness which interacts with the energy.

We have arrived calmly and reasonably at that point of breathtaking surprise, at which we discover that science and God are no longer opposed. Science, after undermining the perhaps already decayed religious dogma of the nineteenth century, is on the verge of reforging our lost connection with the Infinite. We are in the midst of the discovery of our participation in the creation and maintenance of the universe. We are about to learn that God is not separate from us, but always accessible, flowing in and out of us. Dare I say we are about to discover that we are God? This sort of speculation is quickly losing the accompaniments of scorn and embarrassment that a few years ago it would have provoked among physicists or psychic researchers. With the materialist, atheist bias of the Soviet world always present, even Zdenek Rejdak, Czechoslovakia's foremost scientist in the paranormal field, has ventured to say that "this research is helping to rehabilitate the basic human values, revealing that the person is not so helpless after all."

We may want to back off from the immensity of the possibilities we've encountered for a moment, just to take a deep breath before plunging into the infinite once again.

While we sit here blinking and yawning, we may permit ourselves to wonder what Ouija has had to say on the subject of its mechanism and the energy that powers its replies. Do different voices of Ouija concur with the scientists, or even with each other, on this matter? They do agree to a remarkable extent, especially considering the widely diverging beliefs and biases and vocabularies of different Ouija operators. The most concise Ouija account of the physical mechanism involved is one delivered by "Stephen," the voice we have already met. Stephen's explanation, spelled out in 1920, hints at many of the research results of the 1970's.

> "What actually happens during the process of communication," says Stephen, "is more like the transmission of a wireless message than anything else in your experience. Our term receiving station is very good not because it is metaphorical, but because it is the exact opposite of metaphorical.
>
> "I communicate by means of a medium quite material. I utilize a force which man does not now understand, but which in time he will. A few years ago men marveled at the ordinary telegraph; now they are reconciled to wireless."
>
> "Do you mean," I asked, "that electricity operates this Ouija board?"
>
> "But surely," Stephen replied, "though not electricity as you now understand it. The atomic force of which I speak might be called magnetic consciousness."

My own queries about how Ouija works have produced messages more akin to William Tiller than to the voice we call Stephen. Always Ouija has emphasized to me that "energy is energy," with ultimately one source no matter how we perceive its manifestation. Ouija has gone on to say to me that everything we see and experience, every rock and action and star and book, *is* energy (rather than just "containing" energy, but being made of something more definite and palpable)—an observation that physicists have been attempting to convey to the rest of us for several years now.

Here my voices from Ouija go on, and here we leave science behind and leap ahead into our next chapter. The words spelled at my Ouija table tell me that everything is energy when my perspective is an intellectual one. Ouija says that when I see through the eyes of my heart, then everything becomes love. Through another perspective, everything is God. Energy, God and love are each all there is in the universe. Science pursues the truth that all is energy. In the next chapter we will bring in every perspective available to us, and with great energy, love and the guidance of the perspective from which God is all, we will explore the geography of the Great Beyond and see what place the Ouija board may have in that land.

CHAPTER NINE

The Geography of the Great Beyond

You know not the full extent of your souls. Your individual selves have their own integrity —and still, they are cells in My body.

—AUTHOR'S OUIJA BOARD, 1975

As I explored the Ouija board's possibilities for the first time, in the same sequence we've followed in this book, I observed a peculiar process at work. My beginning questions at the board were simple and usually personal, and covered all the topics I've already suggested for first questions. The pointer's answers began with yeses and no's, but soon included such confusions as "maybe," "sometimes," or "yes" *and* "no" given for the same question. It was at this point that I began to examine my questions, to root up the beliefs on which the questions were built and then to question the beliefs. Gradually my use of words became more exact and my beliefs more consciously held, aided by the dependable feedback of the Ouija board, each day showing me just where I was.

As this process went on, my questions to Ouija contained fewer and fewer hidden assumptions, fewer unquestioned or unconscious beliefs, fewer contradictions and much less overt "content." If last month's question had been "What past reincarnation is most affecting the life I live now?" then this month I might say, "Ouija, tell me what I need to know today." My attitude at the Ouija board, through this naturally occurring process, became gradually much quieter, calmer, *emptier. I* provided less and less of the content of the board's messages; I created less and less static, or junky noise, at the board. It took me several months of Ouija experimentation to realize that a process was at work in which, as my "noise" subsided, something else did indeed fill the vacuum. I was in the midst of a shift facilitated by Ouija from *relative* truths—those details of my life that find their meanings in *relation* to me—to what I've since admitted is a realm of *absolute* truth—those details of the workings of the universe that remain true *no matter what* anyone thinks or feels or tries to do about them.

For as long as I could, I continued to think of the Ouija board as an almost mechanical tool that showed me parts of myself and could not cause me any great surprise. Laurel and I pursued "energy" as our Ouija topic, in much the same spirit as current scientists of the paranormal pursue the subject, looking for how energy works and viewing it is a primarily physical phenomenon. Then, in one afternoon's Ouija session, the little board upset our game and showed us we were exploring a realm both larger and closer to home than we had dared imagine. The board's unasked for and, to be honest, unwanted, message was this:

> Hold in your minds all you have learned of energy, and listen: energy is love; love is energy; energy is all there is; love is all there is; energy is love is God.

I saw immediately that this statement did not originate in my beliefs. In fact, I saw that if I were to really believe this message, my life would change in large ways. My personality's defense mechanisms, my attempts at building "security," everything I did in order to be "safe," all of it would be wasted energy, love not given, God denied. Laurel's reaction was similar: "Wait just a minute—I don't think I want to hear about God from the Ouija board." We boycotted Ouija for a few days, 'til curiosity and the emotional distancing of time passing cleared our defenses and readied us for more. In the meantime I had read through the notes from our Ouija sessions with a new ear for the passages about energy. I came away from the notes with the slightly uncomfortable hunch that though it may have been in our own best interests, some trick had been played on Laurel and me. A definite progression *had* been made in our Ouija sessions, from those first straightforward yeses and no's to answers and unrequested messages, each session a little bit further from the beliefs about reality Laurel and I consciously held, 'til finally the pointer triumphantly let us in on the fact that God was the real subject of these lessons.

I have since become reconciled to the fact that it is some larger-than-everyday part of *myself* that plays such tricks in order to teach the small earthbound me. In some ways this idea can be difficult to live with, and we'll touch on those difficulties later, but at least with this concept we don't have a being *separate* from us playing tricks that may not be beneficial to us. This knowledge does nothing to lessen my everyday questions and struggles; it merely keeps my fear of God down to the level of my fear of myself.

Even now, after quite a lot of practice, it's not easy for me to speak of "absolute truth," or its personalized equivalent, God, for several reasons. I suspect that my reasons will echo many of yours, so I'll list them here. Most obvious is that it's not exactly fashionable these days to talk of God at all from personal experience. Anything remotely resembling personal communication with God through the Ouija board has a positively dangerous ring to it, even to my ears. Having a direct Ouija line to Absolute Truth is just as bad. One of my first thoughts after the session in which Ouija equated energy with love, with God, was, "What will people think of our Ouija experiments now?"

I didn't want friends to assume I'd just stepped into the lunatic's Great Beyond (and I continue, sporadically, to hope that *readers* will not, from that same conclusion, jump off this train of thought before its destination is reached).

These fears are fairly easily laid aside (though they may reappear and be laid aside a thousand times), because no matter how ridiculous or ill-informed or gullible or wrong anyone finds us, we still must ultimately come back to our own perceptions and define our experience for ourselves. This brings us to a more serious difficulty in our attempt to look Absolute Truth in the face. How can *we* know we are not being duped by our own pride and self-righteousness into seeing God in what is really just one more set of beliefs? I'm not immune or inexperienced here, and I imagine that most who risk using Ouija so far out to sea will occasionally be dunked under by a sudden swell and have to climb back onto the Ouija raft soggy and embarrassed. This occupational hazard of deep-sea Ouija fishing actually functions most often as a safeguard that keeps pride and self-importance from growing to blinding size, so it isn't really such a fearful possibility after all. We'll make no grandiose blunders, nothing on the scale of those Alaskan ladies who found Ouija to be "God's true and only telegraph to eternity," so long as we continue the attitudes we've cultivated at the Ouija table all along, listening as clearly as we can to what Ouija tells us and *questioning*, always questioning, the board's messages *and* our own reactions, motivations, thoughts, desires. I suggest a periodic renewal of this evaluation process, which you can easily do by rereading the first four chapters of this book along with your own notes on past Ouija sessions.

There is one more danger especially associated with receiving descriptions of God, or bits of Absolute Truth, whether it be with the aid of the Ouija board or by any other method. We are so often inclined to mistake the description for the real thing; we forget that the words and concepts are merely suggestions meant to lead us toward a personal *experience* of God or to catalyze such an experience in someone else who hears the words. Descriptions of the Great Beyond can serve us as reminders, signposts, crudely drawn maps that can never be totally accurate but are better than no map at all. When I finally found the nerve to seriously ask "Is Ouija really God?" the pointer's answer was "To varying degrees, yes—though *always* connected to your temporal beings and so *always* distorted." This same sort of distortion accounts not only for differing Ouija descriptions of the Absolute, but for differences in the world's religions as well. These differing distortions needn't be viewed only negatively, as deviations from "the right description" of the Great Beyond; they can be seen also as personalized maps, containing exactly "the right distortions" to enable a particular individual or culture to actually find the experience of God. The board's great advantage, as I've said many times already, is that it can provide us with completely personalized maps of the Great Beyond.

This praise of individual distortion is not meant to convince us that there is no hierarchy of value, that any Ouija message is as true as any other. We are walking steadily into the land Beyond, and the path is as wide as a knife edge and as sharp as any paradox. The path itself is not made of words or concepts, though a map of words can lead us there. My map may help you draw your own but it can't move you even one step; for real movement, each of us must create our own map and step along the narrow path on our own feet. Sharing and comparing maps of the Great Beyond is important and helpful—most helpful when we remember that the accuracy of the map lies not in its content but in the living experience from which it emerged and toward which it leads us.

As we look at descriptions of this land, at maps of the Absolute stemming from voices of Ouija, our hearts become our most important sensing instruments. Here we can see the necessity of the entire spectrum of Ouija experience we've followed in this book: from our first curiosities, through our gradually growing awareness of our beliefs, to the shifting and loosening of beliefs that occur naturally as we become more conscious of our motivations and thoughts, to the slow emptying of personal concerns at the Ouija board. All this clears our hearts of debris, which in turn makes a space for clearer, more truthful Ouija words *and* for our more accurate appraisal of those words. Our seat of judgment moves from head to heart and the medium of worth turns from logic to love. As one message at my Ouija board put it: "You are conductors for My knowledge. The clarity of transmission will depend on your clarity of love and empathy."

With all this in mind and heart we can profitably take a look at maps of the Great Beyond drawn at various Ouija boards. What I have done with these maps has been to lay them in a stack as if they were transparencies. Then I've looked through the stack, seeing the lines of mountain and ocean in each map all at once. In some places the maps' features have diverged into separate colored squiggles of meanings; in others the lines of meaning collide to form single points that line up exactly all the way through the stack. The features I will emphasize as elements of the Great landscape Beyond are those concepts that have co-incided in every Ouija report. This map will be a very sketchy one with many blank areas owing to the small space we have in which to draw it here, but even so you may notice that the geography described is not unique to Ouija, but shares many landmarks with occult and religious traditions the world over, as well as sharing much with modern science. Those connections will be left undrawn, for you to make if you wish, as our emphasis in these pages will continue on its personal and experiential course.

Our first clue about the nature of the Absolute is contained in the board's insistence that love, or God, or energy, is *all there is*. The voice of Ouija called Stephen explained that *consciousness* is all there is; he said that physical matter is an *attribute* of consciousness, as are time and space. What we call God, Stephen called the "supreme degree of consciousness," which is "composed at once of the height of individual consciousness and of the perfection of individual adjustment to the whole." The voice of Ouija called Patience Worth found another way to make the same statement: "Thou art of Him, aye, and I be of Him, and ye be of Him, and He be all of all."

The voices are emphatic and unanimous in their insistence that we *are* God (or energy or consciousness or love), and that everything we experience as the "real world"—the passing of time, the weather, mountains, traffic jams—all are attributes of God, ways that consciousness has found to express itself. When I first came upon this landmark of the Beyond I felt at once a recognition from some little-known part of me that truth did indeed live here, while at the same time I experienced a sense of uneasiness as a flood of questions came through me. Does individual integrity remain when we are all aspects of God? What place has evil in such a universe? If I'm God why don't I know it? And on and on. Fortunately the signposts pointing toward answers for these questions coincide remarkably for the various voices of Ouija we've met. My questioning thus led to a more thorough understanding of this universe in which we think and breathe, while the understanding gained led back to immense wonder at the mystery of this home of ours.

We've already been given one hint on the subject of individuality from Stephen's description of "supreme consciousness." Somehow individuality is absorbed into God—"individual adjustment to the whole"—and at the same time not diminished at all—"the height of individual consciousness." The truth and importance of individuality is stressed elsewhere in Stephen's messages, and in the statements of other voices as well. Patience Worth says, in a style so characteristic it illustrates her point, "Thou art ye, and I be me and ye be ye, aye, ever so." The voices of Ouija definitely concur on the "ever so," insisting that each individual consciousness (not only each *human* consciousness, but each individual amoeba and stone and fruitfly consciousness) lives forever in its individualized form, whether that form be manifesting physically or not.

This is difficult to comprehend in the same breath as the board's statement of the truth of reincarnation and evolution of consciousness, but with some effort we *can* encompass both aspects of the one reality. The voices of Ouija tell us that the popular conception of reincarnation is half a truth. Though we do experience many lives on this planet, learning from each one and eventually becoming conscious of the unchanging reality behind the many manifestations, it is also true that each incarnation houses a distinct, unique being who will live on *in its present form* beyond this brief physical appearance. Jane Roberts, a prolific psychic explorer who began with the Ouija board, has offered the picture of a self shaped like a wheel with a hub and spokes. Out on one of the spokes is the person you know yourself to be in this lifetime. Other spokes lead to what we call past or future incarnations. They are all linked at the hub, at which point resides a larger self who oversees and perhaps coordinates all the incarnations, and who is focused primarily in some other-than-physical existence.

All this becomes much easier to imagine if we can set aside our conceptions of time and space as solid, unchangeable givens of the universe. Physicists and, more recently, biologists, astronomers and other scientists, have accustomed themselves to empty matter and unstable time in order to be in accord with their findings about the universe. The rest of us will follow sooner or later—sooner, if we are to live with the paradoxes given us through Ouija. Stephen made a good beginning on a simple explanation of the relativity of time and space:

Time and space are attributes of consciousness. Consciousness, being a pluralistic oneness in process of evolution, is, as your everyday experience tells you, necessarily a thing of relationships. Those relationships that are evolutional you know temporally. Those that result from the pluralistic character of the whole you know spatially. As attributes of consciousness time and space are real, as reason or will or form is real. But time and space do not mean to you what they mean to an insect. Nor do they mean to supreme consciousness what they mean to you.

So, we begin to understand that, as we are now, we live "forever," while at the same "time" we also evolve through many lifetimes 'til we become conscious of everything and so are God in the fullest sense. This paradox works because the quality that is time operates in different ways as it passes through different aspects of the universe. Only within this matrix we call the physical world do time and space dictate that future follows present follows past, or that we can be in only one place at one time. Many Ouija board attempts have been made at describing the behavior of time and space as they exist beyond our physical world, but I haven't yet heard a coherent description. Translation here is very difficult; what Ouija can do more easily than spelling is lead us toward actually experiencing bits and pieces of the Beyond. A moment's experience in this realm can bring more understanding than any amount of clumsy word juggling. Still, the words can sometimes lead us to the edge of experience, so we'll continue marking out our maps with them.

The place of evil in our Great Beyond is another sort of paradox: it *seems* to exist, we can find examples of actions that appear to be evil any time we care to look for them, yet in an ultimate, Absolute sense, evil does not exist. Ouija explanations of evil showed themselves in Chapter Four, so I won't repeat them here, though the concept is an important one on our maps of this strange land that is our home. The idea that evil is simply the nondevelopment of good—an absence that receives all its apparent power from our attention to it, whether that attention be focused on spreading evil or combatting it—this concept echoes through every deeply pursued Ouija experience I've encountered.

Let's see what sort of universe this small map has so far described. It is not really a place, our universe, just as I am not a blue eye, since eyes or place are just one attribute among many. Our universe is energy, dancing its transmuting, constantly moving, evolutionary dance, in which every movement and every tiniest variation is remembered and used and no energy is ever lost or destroyed. We ourselves and everything we see and touch or even imagine are this energy, scattered across many realities and individualized in order to create all possible expressions of itself. Here is God. I am That I am.

Within this web of energy we find the small planet we call home, the whole world of physical phenomena, the conventions of solidity and time and distance, our bodies and minds and hearts woven into one "lifetime," which we agree begins with conception or birth and ends with the body's death—everything we all agree to call the "real" world. However, our agreements do not limit the universe's depth and complexity in the least; we have merely succeeded in limiting our own perception of what is. The world we think we know is one grain of sand on one white beach at the edge of the universe's ocean. There is that much more.

Time, space, evil, love, and we ourselves are among the phenomena we have perceived so narrowly that the largest portion of their reality has remained opaque to us. In evil's instance, the larger reality we've missed is an emptiness, an absence. Time and space are realities much more dynamic and creative than we usually imagine them. Love is the largest reality of them all, for rather than being one of many emotions, rather even than being an attribute of God as time or matter are, love *is* God. Love *is* the universe, as God or consciousness is the universe. To whatever extent we love, we become God manifesting in the world; we act as channels for the flow of the energy that is the universe.

Now it may be clear why I said our hearts would become our most valuable sensing instruments as we ventured into the Great Beyond. Love—not the romantic and sentimental love that wants to possess, but the pure giving we've all experienced somewhere that accepts totally and asks nothing in return—this energy is the vehicle that can carry us into the presence of God. Love is the knife-edge path we walk. It slices easily through our perception of evil, because *when we love* we are not focusing our attention on evil, and without our attention evil has no fuel. Love can alter our perceptions of time and space, stretching time 'til it becomes a connector rather than a separator, and condensing our experience of space to the same end. When we love *ourselves*, the knife's edge cuts through our beliefs about our own separateness, our guilt, our unworthiness, and we are allowed to glimpse our connection with that larger self who we really are, the one who always knows she is God.

Some people have a gift for loving fully, and for them no other tool is necessary in the exploration of the Great Beyond. For others of us, intellectual tools can be very helpful in leading us toward understanding. There are two such intellectual tools mentioned by every voice of Ouija and especially stressed by Stephen. The first is the truth Stephen called "the law of parallels"—the idea of the correspondence between macrocosm and microcosm, most simply stated in the ancient Chinese expression, "As above, so below." We can see this principle manifested even in the physical world: the spiral of a certain molecule is the spiral of the seed arrangement at a sunflower's center, is the same spiral in the seashell's anatomy and the spiral also of our galaxy in its movement. This is connection by synchronicity rather than by cause and effect. In the same way, the glimmers of the Absolute we have been shown through these many Ouija voices will prove to be true in actual application on any scale. My presentation has been abstract in order to cover a wide field of experience and bring in as few of my own distortions as possible; translating these truths into the practical issues of the lives we live now is a work each of us must do for herself.

The other important tool we have been given to guide us

in our journey is the truth of evolution. We have become accustomed to seeing evolution's truth in the physical world, à la Darwin. Now, using the tool we've called the law of parallels, we can see the evolution of physical form as a small example of a much larger process. Physical forms evolve in order that consciousness itself may evolve. As Stephen emphasized: "Evolution is an actuality more potent than earth theorists have dreamed." We cannot help but become more conscious. Our choices lie simply in whether we will drag our feet and so evolve more slowly, or spread those not-yet-formed wings and prepare to fly.

It is at this point, with the addition of "the two great glimpses," as Stephen called them, that our map of the Great Beyond *almost* touches back down onto the ground of science, left behind last chapter. If scientists were willing to extend their own use of the laws of correspondence and evolution from the study of physical matter into the study of consciousness, our flight into metaphysics could be more easily seen for what it is, namely, a short tour over the One Reality we all share. Actually, as you read these words, just such an extension of science into what has been called God is being made manifest. The connective work is as yet too theoretical for mention in our chapter on how Ouija works; it is too complicated to give more than mention to it here. The first public hint of such an enormously important shift in science's focus came in 1977 with the simultaneous and separate presentation of a new model of the universe by three scientists. They are David Bohm, a physicist at the University of London, Karl Pribram, a Stanford University brain researcher, and Itzhak Bentov, an independent inventor whose specialty is biomedical engineering. Central to all of their theories is the tenet that everything, including all matter, *is* consciousness. The physical world, in all three theories, is said to be a holographic projection constructed from elements of "a realm of meaningful, patterned primary reality that transcends time and space." Bohm and Pribram published their theories in scientific journals; Itzhak Bentov presented his as a delightfully simple book for the person who knows nothing of physics or biology. It is called *Stalking the Wild Pendulum: On the Mechanics of Consciousness* (published in paperback by E. P. Dutton, 1977). I recommend it highly as a technical companion to this book. Without intending to, Bentov makes Ouija adventure much more rationally accessible to those of us who feel a need for that sort of explanation.

We near the end of this small trailblazing excursion across the universe that we are, but that we don't know. For some reader, the most important feature on our map will be the truth of evolution's power. For someone else, a glimpse of evil's limitations will be most important. In every case, the importance lies in the concept's ability to facilitate changes in the way we view *ourselves*. "So I *am* changing for the better, perhaps in spite of myself," our first reader might say. No matter how far out into the cosmos we seem to have gone, from where we sit *here* the significant journey is also an inward one.

The landmarks and signposts we've encountered on this tour through the land Beyond are not offered as points of doctrine. No, my only purpose in setting these glimpses before you has been to reach your hearts somehow, to strike a resonant chord with my words in order that you may *experience* the truth that lies dormant within the words. The words, the concepts, are important only as they bring us to that point of direct experience in which, if only for a moment so brief it has no measure, we know the universe directly, we *are* God. After even one such moment your life will never be quite the same again; you will never again be able to totally believe in your limitations and shortcomings. (While at first glance this may seem no loss at all, I've found I sometimes have a tremendous resistance to giving up my faults and admitting that I'm God.)

Ouija can be the gentlest of guides in our movement toward more fully experiencing the universe we create and inhabit. The voices at my Ouija board once described the process we undergo there in this way:

Entirely up to you be the words of this message, and yet the meanings come from across the Beyond. Be assured of the verity of communication. Keep the conversation going and you will find our meanings come clearer and your words become more exact. We will teach you not through using your minds or speaking through you, but by allowing you to glimpse ever more accurate and complete vistas of the one reality, which you must form into articulacies of your own making. This way the regulation or timing will be your own; the impetus will be yours and the accomplishments too.

The real journey into the Being we are right now, the deep mystery we've been calling the Great Beyond, must be undertaken by each of us individually. Though our maps show the same landmarks and we follow the same sequence at our talking boards, what each of us finds in that land is for us alone. One day as you sit at the Ouija board, some small surprise it brings dazzles you and only you, and alone you drop your habits of perception, you forget the usual way you create the moment-to-moment world. As you grope for your habits in the wake of surprise, you glimpse a flash of silver embroidery on a turquoise hem, and spinning a glance round your shoulder you see for an instant that it is *your* garment so finely woven. You look up and it is gone. You sit again in a familiar apartment bedroom, dressed as usual in jeans and T-shirt and half-smiling now, confusion mixed with wonder. You shrug and return your fingers to the Ouija pointer, and these words are spelled:

Tentative moves are being acted out by portions of yourselves now in far galaxies—the results are forming your futures in this one. Nowhere are your essences not known. You are not the small creatures you fancy yourselves to be. Parts of you inhabit every corner of your universe—which is not, by the way, the only one.

CHAPTER TEN

Leaving the Ouija®
Board Behind

When you once get hold of anything of this
sort so it is inside you, at once it begins to work
automatically, so you don't have to fuss with it.

—"The Invisibles," 1937

We've come a long way in this small book. Whether we began with curiosity or near indifference, with fear or great expectations about what might be delivered to us at the Ouija board, we've all come to realize by now that, with every possible use of the little board, Ouija remains a tool through which *we change.* Not only that, but our changes follow a certain course that transforms us into ever more definite and clear beings—definite in our beliefs and free of the excess baggage of worn-out convictions, clear in our perceptions of the world without and within us. We have by now either experienced for ourselves or seen by the light of this book that Ouija not only propels us through all these changes, but does so in order to enable us to enter into conversation with the Great Beyond. Since we are the

Great Beyond, and the Great Beyond is God, we can say that Ouija is a tool through which we enter into conversation with the parts of ourselves that are God, the parts of us that reach beyond our conscious selves into the infinite one reality that is God. Ouija is a tool through which we become more and more conscious that we are God. Let's say it in the bluntest way possible: the Ouija board is a tool through which we become God.

We know when our Ouija conversation has entered the infinite not especially by the words that are spelled, but by the way we feel, by the way our hearts resonate to the words of Ouija. If the board's words bring love with them, if they leave us feeling a deeper and more thorough love than we felt before, then we know we've been in contact with the infinite. If a Ouija session doesn't leave love in its wake, that's fine too. Since love is all there is, when we don't find love at our Ouija table we know we're dealing with something that doesn't really exist, some distortion of the Absolute that finds its home in our beliefs. We listen to such voices, we change ourselves by their guidance, knowing them for what they are and are not.

The purpose of Ouija is to prepare us for communication with the Absolute, and then to introduce us. Once such a connection has been established from our "blindered" world into that unlimited One, the key to communication remains *in us*. The Ouija board itself is not the key. Our hearts hold the key to contact with the Great Beyond; all we need is to *feel* a clear connection once and we can return. The experience of contact with our infinite Selves actually creates neural pathways in our bodies that had not existed before and that we can then use to reconnect with the Beyond—so say the voices who now speak to me sans the Ouija board.

Once we have learned through Ouija to communicate with our larger selves, those infinite beings in whom we have our home may choose to wean us from the board and pointer. By now we know that the Ouija board itself is nothing, that the ability to reach out to the infinite and find ourselves there lies in our own bodies and minds, so the task of communicating with the Beyond *without* the Ouija board has become at least an imaginable further step.

Of Ouija adventurers we've heard from in this book—Hester Travers Smith, Pearl Curran, who brought us "Patience Worth," Darby and Joan with "Stephen," Betty and Stewart White—every one of them left the Ouija board behind at some point in their exploration and continued to receive information from their voices of Ouija by more direct means. Many other psychic explorers started their development with Ouija or planchette, but graduated so quickly to hearing the words directly or speaking from a trance state that they left no substantial Ouija work to mention in these pages.

In every case the weaning process follows a unique and often peculiar course prescribed by the individual's voices (and here I refer only to those voices our hearts claim as their own, as messengers from the infinite Heart). *Your* voices received from Ouija, speaking at first through the little board, will tell you if, when and especially *how* to move from the board's method to another one more direct.

Sometimes the progression is a swift one. As an example, Betty White used the Ouija board only once; its only message was to tell her over and over, "Get a pencil." She did get a pencil and began to write automatically, a procedure she followed at regular sessions for several months in the presence of her partner, Stewart White. The writing stopped when it had said it would; in its place Betty began to go on excursions into the Beyond, in which, while her body lay at rest, she experienced the lessons of "the Invisibles" as real journeys through time and space, complete with sights, sounds, smells and bodily sensations. She recounted these experiences to Stewart, often as they were happening, and Stewart took notes and provided a stability to which she could return. In some important way Betty and Stewart White remained Ouija partners; both were essential to their method's success. In terms of Chapter One's discussion of Ouija pairs, Betty was the receptive

or positive partner, the one whose mind received and translated the incoming information; Stewart's role, beyond his
duties as scribe, was to supply additional biophysical energy.

Contemporary psychic explorer Jane Roberts followed a
course similar to Betty White's. Both women initiated their
contact with the Beyond through the Ouija board and went
quickly on to other methods. In Jane's instance, the words
began to appear in her mind before they were spelled at the
board, so to save time she began to speak them aloud. Soon
not only words but an entire personality, with its own ges-
tures and inflections of voice, was speaking through Jane.
(The books dictated by this personality, who is called Seth,
continue to be widely available and I highly recommend
any of them, as well as Jane Robert's own more recent
books dealing with her other psychic adventures.) Jane
Roberts carries on these dictations from Seth with the help
of her husband, Robert Butts, in a working arrangement
almost exactly the same as the method worked out by Betty
and Stewart White. Darby and Joan also developed the
same arrangement for their work, though they stayed with
the Ouija board for a much longer time before trying any
innovations.

Pearl Curran stayed with the Ouija board for a full seven
years before finally setting it aside. In 1918, after five years
of Patience Worth's productions at the board, Pearl began
to know each letter before the pointer spelled it. Soon she
was reciting the letters as they came to her, while the
pointer circled aimlessly. In 1920, shortly before setting
aside the board and pointer for the last time, Pearl wrote
this:

> I am rapidly discarding the Ouija board. This has been
> coming on for a long time. For months I have been almost
> unconsciously dropping the spelling of the words until I
> have been able lately to simply recite the poems instead;
> though if I become conscious of the change, I have to go
> back to the spelling. . . . I expect eventually to discard the
> board altogether.

My own evolution from Ouija beginnings has so far taken a path much less dramtic than that of any of these ladies with their personalitied voices received from Ouija. My experience is likely to be a common one so I'll relate it here. After several months of Ouija experimentation, I began to know letters before they were spelled, and then to know whole words and phrases. I refused to believe at first that the words appearing in my mind were really the words the Ouija pointer intended to spell, so I kept my mouth shut and made the pointer continue on its course. It always spelled the words I knew it would spell. Then I seized the thought that since I knew the words first, they must originate in my conscious mind and therefore I must be manipulating the Ouija board in a crass and almost conscious fashion. I felt disgusted with the whole enterprise. Eventually, though, I learned to *quiet my thoughts* much more than before, and from that quietness I could feel the origin of the smaller volume of words flowing through my mind. I learned to distinguish different qualities of Ouija words from each other and from "my own" thoughts. Somewhere along the way I discovered that *no* thoughts originate in our conscious minds; they all come from somewhere else and are amplified into our awareness. I went back to the Ouija board, using it now as a way to focus my attention and keep me on course as I said the words aloud, checking now and then with the pointer when I was unsure what came next.

What did come next was the pointer's suggestion that I set aside the Ouija board and speak its words directly. I did not gracefully oblige. Rather, I felt very threatened and frightened by the prospect, as I saw it, of setting aside not only the Ouija board but my very own personality and conscious self, while some stranger inhabited my throat. This reaction may seem extreme and paranoid, and it is, but it is also common.

It was at this point that I realized I would never venture further into the Beyond, or let the Unknown enter me, until I had moved further in two directions. One, I obviously did not believe I lived in a safe universe; I had to remake my beliefs about the Beyond until they could no longer hurt me. At the same time, there had to be less of *me* to be hurt. I needed to empty my personality still further, eventually down to the point at which there'd be *nothing of me to lose* in the infinite. In such a state, the information I brought back would be distorted as little as is possible for any human making the transition from the infinite to this consensual world.

This is the stage at which I find myself now, still emptying that which is not true in myself, still creating the universe in which I can safely travel. I am still learning to listen for the voice of my larger self, still learning to distinguish what is true from what is interesting or almost true or what I most want to hear. I go back to the Ouija board for encouragement and clarity, and to play at specific projects like the mysterious novel of Ouija. I've found that the truest Ouija voices come to me quietly and unannounced, so I make a quiet unobtrusive space in myself where they will always feel welcome, and I turn my ear to that space often to find out what the voices have to say. It's nothing dramatic. The voices not only do not boom—they make no sound at all, just the stillness of knowing, which I then articulate as best I can into the fabric of my life.

If you feel a need for specific advice about this matter of bringing the authority of your infinite self into everyday life, try the words of Betty White's "Invisibles." Their teachings, directed at Stewart White and, especially, Betty, were published in 1937 as *The Betty Book*. The book has recently been reissued in paperback by E. P. Dutton. And —need I say it?—remember your talking board. You may want to stay with the little board through your whole life, or come back to it only when you're stuck somewhere between here and the Beyond, or you may want to use it regularly in addition to other tools and other methods. Let your truest and most loving voices of Ouija guide you.

Now I've shared with you all I know about Ouija. We are equals from this point on, fellow adventurers standing at the edge of the world. My knees shake as I peer over the cliff's edge looking for some clue, but all I see is a slowly moving fog bank far below, obscuring the already impenetrable distance. A shudder goes through me and then a deep breath as I lose my fearful concentration and begin instead to savor our common predicament. I turn to you and smile, my carefully chosen words of encouragement evaporating on my lips. You don't need my encouragement. God cannot help but go with you.

Brenda Alexander
plane 3 unit
fr June 1956.